Education for Knowing

Education for Knowing

Theories of Knowledge for Effective Student Building

Paul A. Wagner and Frank K. Fair

ROWMAN & LITTLEFIELD
Lanham • Boulder • New York • London

Published by Rowman & Littlefield
An imprint of The Rowman & Littlefield Publishing Group, Inc.
4501 Forbes Boulevard, Suite 200, Lanham, Maryland 20706
www.rowman.com

6 Tinworth Street, London SE11 5AL, United Kingdom

Copyright © 2021 by Paul A. Wagner and Frank K. Fair

All rights reserved. No part of this book may be reproduced in any form or by any electronic or mechanical means, including information storage and retrieval systems, without written permission from the publisher, except by a reviewer who may quote passages in a review.

British Library Cataloguing in Publication Information Available

Library of Congress Cataloging-in-Publication Data

Names: Wagner, Paul A., 1947– author. | Fair, Frank K., 1944– author.
Title: Education for knowing : theories of knowledge for effective student building / Paul A. Wagner, Frank K. Fair.
Description: Lanham : Rowman & Littlefield, [2020] | Includes bibliographical references and index. | Summary: "If our goal is Education for Knowing, as the title says, then we need to be guided by a conception of what knowing is. For example, we can all agree that there are "math facts" that students need to learn, and we can agree that there are general concepts and laws that students should be acquainted with. But is there more involved, perhaps something like nurturing in students a desire to probe deeper into the workings of things? Or developing a capacity to explain why things work the way they do? Our conceptions of what genuine knowing is serve as guides to what we think the goal of education is, and they tell us how to "build a student." However, as it turns out, there are multiple conceptions of what knowing truly involves, and these conceptions tend to be different for different sets of education stakeholders such as parents and their children, school administrators, and educational researchers. Understanding this diversity of conceptions of knowing will make it easier for representatives of the different stakeholder groups to work together to accomplish the goal of building knowing students"— Provided by publisher.
Identifiers: LCCN 2020035515 (print) | LCCN 2020035516 (ebook) | ISBN 9781475848137 (hardcover) | ISBN 9781475848144 (paperback) | ISBN 9781475848151 (ebook)
Subjects: LCSH: Education—Aims and objectives. | Knowledge, Theory of.
Classification: LCC LB41 .W16 2020 (print) | LCC LB41 (ebook) | DDC 370.11—dc23
LC record available at https://lccn.loc.gov/2020035515
LC ebook record available at https://lccn.loc.gov/2020035516

Paul Wagner would like to dedicate this work to Jeanene, my lovely wife and spiritual partner, and to Jason, my most loyal son, of whom I am so very proud.

Frank Fair would like to dedicate this book to his wife Janet, who had to bear many burdens while he was working on it, to our now-grown children, Ken and Joanna, who are working to make the world a better place, and, most of all, to our grandchildren, Nathan, Emma, and Emily, who already make the world a better place simply because they are in it.

Contents

Preface		ix
Acknowledgments		xiii
Introduction		xv
1	Conceptions of Knowledge I: Realism versus Skepticism	1
2	Why Children and Their Parents Are Natural Realists	13
3	Conceptions of Knowledge II: Contextualism and Pragmatism	33
4	Policy-Makers and Administrators as Contextualists and Pragmatists	47
5	Conceptions of Knowledge III: Instrumentalism, Evidentialism, and Social Constructionism	67
6	Educational Researchers as Instrumentalists, Evidentialists, or Social Constructionists	85
7	Bringing the Perspectives Together	101
8	Sketching a Path Forward	119
Glossary		141
References		147
Index		161
About the Authors		167

Preface

It is tempting to say that this book is about educational researchers, administrators, and instructors saying what they know. But that would be misleading. The authors' ambitions run deeper than that. How deep?

There is something called the theory of knowledge or *epistemology* from the Greek. It is the study of how people can justify what they say is true or claim to know. Because we all know that people, including ourselves, can make mistakes, and that every day we make judgments about what we—and others—really know or do not know, this sort of study is older than written history can report.

So, around the world, scholars and ordinary people want the matter settled. When the mechanic says to the customer, "You need a new transmission," the customer wants to know whether the mechanic knows what she is talking about. But how does the mechanic know?

When the teacher tells a child's parents that their son or daughter needs to apply himself or herself more to the study of geometry, the parents want to know how the teacher knows that this is true.

When a famed researcher such as the developmental psychologist Jean Piaget tells other researchers that a child of a certain early age typically does not know that when the liquid in a tall, skinny container is poured into a short, fat container, it is still the same amount, those other researchers want to know how Piaget knows what he claims to know. How does he *know* rather than simply *believe*?

The answers to all these sorts of questions have tempted theorists and practitioners alike to do one of three things. First, they may scurry about and try to conjure up a theory covering all claims to know the truth. This would be a theory of justification.

With regard to defining the truth, the logician Alfred Tarski did this when he gave us an example that represents all of the true statements we might make. His example was simply this: "The sentence 'Snow is white' is true IF AND ONLY IF snow is white." That sounds dandy. But what if we cannot agree on what counts as snow? What if we cannot agree on what counts as white? And, even more, just what is the proper relationship between truth and knowledge? So problems lurk even in otherwise simple examples, such as claiming a common object has a certain color, and things are not as simple as they may first appear.

Second, some try to circumvent the challenge of explaining how they know. The iconic educational theorist John Dewey did this by distinguishing between truth and instrumental value. Dewey initially sought a theory of justification for making truth claims, but, failing to find an adequate theory, he proposed a default position: If a description or plan of action leads us to successfully achieve the purpose we have in a given context, then we have all of the justification needed. This sounds good. But, what happened to the idea of truth?

The third effort comes from skeptics who have pos-modern sympathies and who become so exercised over what seems to them the futility of the search for truth or knowledge that they end up urging us to cease the effort entirely. Instead, they argue that we should be content to settle for social agreement. What this means is that they have become skeptical about any sort of truth as well as any demonstrably correct resolution to a query of any sort. These thoroughgoing skeptics instead proclaim that "everyone has his or her own truths." We hear echoes of this view when the notion of "alternative facts" is bandied about. Social agreement is what drives every action and intellectual description or planning effort— not any accord with reality.

For these theorists, simple belief—whether collective or individual—becomes the final default position. However, people in education who are responsible for policy, educational researchers, and classroom teachers want something more to secure their professional practices. Theorists from Plato in ancient times to Harvey Siegel, Gwen Bradford, and Catherine Elgin in our time have tried to provide these stakeholders with some overarching theory to ground responsible practice.

While we have learned from their work and appreciate its value, the approach of this book is different. We offer no overarching theory of knowledge, but instead explain that in the practices of education, research, and policy-making, a *pluralistic approach* to justifying knowledge claims makes sense. It makes sense, that is, as long as it allows for constructing bridges between various groups of stakeholders.

When you finish reading this book, we would like you to have both a sound understanding of how to justify knowledge claims in your professional work as well as an understanding of how your justifications can be accommodated by stakeholders at other levels.

Acknowledgments

Paul A. Wagner: There truly are too many to mention. These few are mentioned as much for their contribution to this particular book as well as to my delight in intellectual adventures generally. First and perhaps foremost are Israel Scheffler, Jacob Getzels, C. J. Lucas, and Patrick Suppes; each gave me a sense that I had a future in this business. Second is my coauthor, who has worked with me previously and graciously continues to do so. Frank Fair has patience and tolerance with one who too often has little of either. I respect Frank for his mind and deft hand with a pen. Finally, thanks to Chris Dede, whose office I now inhabit, as he left for what eventually became an endowed chair at Harvard CSE.

Frank Fair: First, there is Joseph John Sikora, SJ, whose invitation to a high school senior English class to read the *Brothers Karamazov* changed me from a physics major into a philosophy major. Later, in graduate school, are Bowman Clarke, who married symbolic logic and philosophy of religion, and Tony Nemetz, whose assignment of a paper on Plato's *Symposium*—one that was to be done by referring to the text alone without citing secondary sources—became (after a couple of incomplete grades) my defining graduate school experience. And thanks to Paul Wagner for inviting me along on this ride after our previous collaborations. Paul and I have worked out a division of labor that makes us both do better work together than we could do apart.

Introduction

A recent *New York Times* list of nonfiction best-sellers includes a book by David Epstein titled *Range: Why Generalists Triumph in a Specialized World* (2019). The title is bound to strike many readers as rather odd. After all, in the age of computer algorithms and greater specialization, especially across the sciences and medicine, it may look as if progress is the exclusive domain of highly practiced experts.

Specialization has its role, Epstein admits. If you are in Australian outback, an Aboriginal guide is likely to be much more useful than a newly minted computer scientist from Carnegie Mellon.

Epstein divides the world between generalists and another group that we choose to call nongeneralists (our, not his, terminology). Generalists have a large reservoir of abstraction, concepts, metaphors, and analogies to call upon when problem-solving, whereas the nongeneralist is bound to the experience of his intellectual locale.

Aboriginal people and many scientists count as nongeneralists. In each case they have learned recipes to apply to a narrowly defined range of experience. Beyond their area of expertise, their recipes and algorithms quickly become less relevant to the demands at hand.

Many intelligent scientists never get beyond the lab or fieldwork, publishing modest confirmations refutations of larger claims. They are not usually the ones to make larger claims. Their education is typically very narrow and prepares them for little beyond their intellectual locale. Epstein claims this is similar to what psychologist Alexander Luria found in villagers he studied in remote Siberia early in the last century (Epstein, 2019).

In contrast, consider the playfulness of the tennis-playing biologist James Watson and physicist Francis Crick. Neither were prepared to study molecular biology. Nonetheless, they found in each other a generalizing mind charmed by novel puzzles. They joined forces at Cavendish Laboratory and eventually published a paper establishing the double helix structure of the DNA molecule.

Chess masters like Garry Kasparov spend a lifetime studying patterns on chess boards. But recipe-following computers were eventually able to master the patterns and recipes. Tiger Woods practiced golf ever since he was two, and it paid off. But these are narrowly defined closed systems. Tennis player Roger Federer did not start tennis until rather late, and yet he mastered the game. Epstein believes tennis is a more open system conducive to a generalist, while golf is more narrowly constrained.

Epstein cites research by Chris Argyris that suggests narrowly specialized experts have brittle personalities and react badly when brought into problem frames for which they are ill-prepared. When put into a generalist environment, non-generalists are often at a loss (Epstein, 2019, p. 30). He goes on to cite psychologist Ellen Winner, saying that no narrow savant has ever become a "Big-C creator" in a field. Epstein adds Rice University Professor Erik Dane's observation that narrow specialization leads to what he calls "cognitive entrenchment." To avoid cognitive entrenchment, Dane recommends "having one foot outside your world" (p. 32).

This brings us to the core rationale for this book. We live in a time when people are increasingly trained in the application of very narrowly contrived strategies for teaching, administrating, and researching. Strict rubric-driven practices and equally strict recipes for ensuring accountability are driving professional educators into nongeneralist thinking. The imagination required for student building and bringing students into the "Great Conversation of Humankind" in sustainable ways is daunting.

Students must learn to do more than memorize and apply recipes in this or that subject. Computers already do that better than humans ever will. Students need to learn how to *understand* and *evaluate* knowledge claims, the application of recipes, and the strategic employment of concepts, skills, and dispositions across intellectual locales.

Obviously, some memorization is necessary; how else could one learn to work with the periodic table, for example? Also, obviously, students must learn the substance of algorithms that are utilized in computers. But there is a necessary caution. Epstein mentions that he completed a master's thesis in a science. He plugged numbers into a computer program, and got a conclusion and, with that, a degree. Only later, as a result of a more general understanding of statistics, did he learn that his thesis was flawed. How else can students learn to understand and evaluate knowledge and plans if they do not understand how knowledge claims are best justified? To build a student and bring her into a lifetime of participation in the Great Conversation of Humankind requires that specialized training always be kept in balance with more generalized preparation in reasoning and engaging others in a community of inquiry. (For an elaboration of this theme, see Wagner et al., 2018)

Epstein refers to a study by James Flynn, who discovered what has come to be called "the Flynn effect." Flynn showed that IQ scores around the world are rising as much as three points every ten years, such that psychometricians have to recalibrate the tests periodically to keep 100 as the middle of the distribution. In a later study, Flynn found that for many students with high grade point averages in their disciplines, "almost none of the students in any major showed a consistent understanding of how to apply methods of evaluating truth they had learned in their own discipline to other areas" (Epstein, 2019, p. 49).

Flynn went on to show that, despite ascending IQ scores and grades, students' scores on tests of critical thinking and their ability to grasp abstract concepts were declining (Epstein, 2019, pp. 47–48). Epstein takes this as further evidence that students are being schooled much like computers are programmed, and that this does little to advance real human intellectual talents, which are best found in critical thinking and the ability to conceive novel abstractions. This means that students do not know and cannot justify what they think they know. So, what is the point?

If students are less and less able to understand or evaluate knowledge claims, whether their own or those of others, then they are not prepared to join in or understand what the Great Conversation of Humankind is all about. Being programmed is not the same as becoming educated. Educated participants are sufficiently general in terms of understanding and in skills and dispositions of evaluation to engage with others in the Great Conversation.

For example, we can debate whether socialism or capitalism is better— but wait! What do we mean by the terms *socialism* and *capitalism*? Could something in between the two economic models be a better goal? How do you *know*?

Simply asserting a claim, even if one can get others to chime in, does not show understanding of the issues at hand. Simply liking a slogan is not grounds for intellectual commitment. To participate with others in the Great Conversation, in addition to embodying the virtues of respect and truth-seeking, participants must understand what it means to know something. They must understand how to justify and evaluate knowledge claims.

Simon Blackburn explains, "Our knowledge of the empirical world starts with the way in which sensory experience is transmuted into confidence in particular propositions" (Blackburn, 2005, p. 47). To know something, in other words, is to go from experience to justified belief through the accuracy of descriptive propositions. This is the balance between specialist and generalist learning that we argue should be sought.

Blackburn wisely notes that "without at least a glimmering of a story about the structure of knowledge and its scope and limits,." intellectual challenges "cannot be tackled" (Blackburn, 2005, p. 43). In the chapters that follow, we intend to show all stakeholders in education how they can develop their own apt theory of knowledge compatible with their professional roles, and how they can understand other sectors of stakeholder practice.

Before proceeding further, let us return one last time to Blackburn's wisdom in the matter of necessary theories of knowledge for any intellectual advancement.

> Challenges ask whether some possibility or other has in fact been ruled out by the evidence. In everyday life many possibilities are merely bare possibilities, too far-fetched to bother with. . . . Visual hallucinations are possible, but in the street the sight of a bus bearing down on me leaves me no time nor inclination to consider whether it is a relevant possibility. Bare possibilities are properly ignored. Real possibilities, on the other hand, defeat claims to know (Blackburn, 2005, p. 46).

Education has been around for millennia. You would think that by now we would have it all figured out. Alas, that is not the case. There is still much to learn, as there is with every aspect of social life and the world beyond our own minds and sensory apparatus. As humans around the world genuinely engage one another in trying to figure out the purpose, nature, and best policy and protocols for pursuing the Great Conversation of Humankind, they are engaged in one aspect of it: education, which focuses on itself.

Over time, locales and practices for parts of the Great Conversation became institutionalized. In the process of becoming institutionalized, the parts of the Great Conversation meant to prepare people for participation became physically localized, first in schools and then in school systems, from preschool to universities and professional schools. Professional educators are to invite and to host participants in the Conversation.

Schooling practices became necessary to provide an enclave for physically hosting the Conversation. Professional managers of schooling began to emerge in the nineteenth century and became professionalized as a class of stakeholders in the twentieth century. Shortly thereafter, another class of professional stakeholders evolved—the educational scientists.

Educational scientists do research on every aspect of school and intellectual life. They study learning, teaching, motivation, nature versus nurture, program evaluation, and research methodology, to name just a few.

The original stakeholder class is still with us, of course, and is made up of teachers, students, parents and, to a lesser extent, the rest of concerned society. For the purposes of this book we will address the theories of knowledge most naturally employed by each of these three groups of stakeholders.

There are many approaches to theories of knowledge, so we can only show in high relief which theories of knowledge are most common in the efforts of stakeholders at three levels. The goal is to give the reader a sense of the driving force behind knowledge claims made in each of the three stakeholder classes.

In addition, we show that once the theory of knowledge in one's own stakeholder group is understood, one can contribute more effectively to understanding and evaluating knowledge claims within that group. And, to the extent that one learns the theory of knowledge prevalent within another stakeholder group, appreciation for and understanding of that group's labors should facilitate communication among the stakeholder groups.

Finally, the book concludes by showing how the stakeholder groups can be brought together by embracing commonly shared values and virtues complementary to provisioning for the Conversation. In this provisioning all stakeholder groups are engaged in what we call *student building*. Many animals are learners, but only humans engage in student building. If everyone in education succeeds, then education becomes a lifetime engagement in the Great Conversation of Humankind.

Technical sketches of the respective theories of knowledge are found in chapters 1, 3, and 5. Following each sketch of a theory of knowledge is a chapter explaining action in light of the previous chapter's focus, which affects the activities of stakeholders at a given level. So, chapter 2 focuses on Level 1 stakeholders, namely teachers, parents, students, and concerned society-at-large. Their leading theory of knowledge is called here *realism*, and it is introduced in chapter 1.

Chapter 4 focuses on theories of knowledge most dominant among Level 2 stakeholders, namely professional educational administrators and policymakers. Their leading theory of knowledge is called *pragmatism* or, sometimes, *instrumentalism*, and that theory is introduced in chapter 3.

Finally, chapter 6 focuses on the most recently evolved theory of knowledge. known as *evidentialism*. It is prominent among Level 3 stakeholders, educational researchers, and is introduced in chapter 5.

Again, keep in mind that these sketches are in high relief, and no stakeholder should be charged with violating the ethos of the stakeholder class if he or she fails to demonstrate card-carrying loyalty to the sketches we outline.

Chapter 7 is meant to show that there are inevitable differences in sense of purpose, and possible difficulties in collaboration among stakeholder groups whose members recklessly follow their own theory of knowledge and disparage the efforts of one or another of the stakeholder groups. These antagonisms are nowhere more evident than in the controversy surrounding *accountability* and programmatic strategies for advancing whatever goes on in the nation's schooling systems.

Chapter 8 brings together an outline for future cooperative success with each theory of knowledge in its place. This is more than a guiding hope. With shared respect for the truth-seeking efforts of each stakeholder group, collaboration is not only possible, but is key to renewed success in our educational and schooling efforts.

We also have provided a short glossary. When an important term is first used in the text, it will appear in bold print. The reader then knows that she can find more about the term by turning to the glossary.

The focus on illuminating the theories of knowledge is not meant to be an ode to optimism. Rather, we present the scaffolding upon which the architecture of successful planning and practice can proceed in the future. The citations cover a broad swath of information, and we hope every reader will take it upon themselves to read works cited in so far as they might apply to the reader's particular interests.

Chapter One

Conceptions of Knowledge I

Realism versus Skepticism

THE IDEAL OF TRUTH: FROM MERE BELIEF TO KNOWLEDGE

Nearly everyone has a theory of knowledge, whether or not they can articulate it. From an early age we all have some degree of *metacognition*—cognition about cognition. A theory of knowledge sorts out those beliefs with the greatest utility from beliefs that have little. Presumably, beliefs have their greatest utility when they more closely approximate truth than to other beliefs considered. Of course, this is not always true, as sometimes mistaken beliefs can lead to much-needed confidence that can help surviving or succeeding in a challenging situation.

Nonetheless, all things being equal, beliefs approximating truth are reasonably favored over those that do not. This is true in the ordinary world most people engage with, as well as in the rarefied world of high-energy physics, which seems to circumvent both common sense and ordinary experience at times. In the end, however, truth is always about what is real. And knowledge always tries to appropriate truth.

THE SEARCH FOR TRUTH HAS AN ANCIENT PEDIGREE

In Greek antiquity, Socrates was infamous among the local authorities in Athens for his propensity for and skill in asking variants of the "How do you know?" question. Socrates did not doubt the existence of truth, but he did doubt that people actually knew what they thought they knew.

Socrates was not a **skeptic**. Quite the contrary, he advised his students: "Know thyself." It is difficult to say what exactly he meant by this, but nonetheless, at the very least it shows that he believed that there are conclusions one can draw about one's self that may be right or wrong.

Plato, a student of Socrates, was certainly one of the first to ever try to elaborate a full theory explaining what it takes to know in order to legitimate a person's claim to know. Plato thought that people can be mistaken about what they observe. Still, there must be an explanation of reality. Plato found himself drawn into metaphysical speculations about the nature of truth. Surely, he reasoned, knowledge must be about what is true. But since human observations are fallible, for a knowledge claim to capture truth, it must extend beyond what is simply observed (Plato, 2004).

Plato concluded that truth was otherworldly, that it went beyond appearances. Knowledge was achieved through thinking long enough and hard enough to envision the truth that exists beyond human senses. Knowledge was right thinking about ultimate reality (Plato, 2004). This amounts to what scholars and scientists now call realism. Authentic knowledge is error-free in such realist thinking. Conclusions that are not wholly true cannot be considered knowledge.

REALISM TODAY

Famous realists who continue working on theory of knowledge today include Lynne Ruder Baker, Hilary Putnam, and many others (Baker, 2007; Putnam, 1990). Realists today generally try to align themselves with something apart from Plato's abstract **metaphysics**. For example, the great logician Alfred Tarski once explained that truth is about representations mapped onto the world without error. So, a sentence such as "Snow is white" is true IF AND ONLY IF snow IS white (Tarski, 1944). If there is any mismatch between the representation and the reality it claims to reveal, then the representation is not true and cannot count as an example of knowledge.

Wait . . . what!

Can there be some sort of *guarantee* in any theory of knowledge that the claimed match exists between reality and the representation said to be knowledge? Can there be a process, perhaps a proof or an experiment, that can guarantee a match between representation and reality? In a word, no (Church, 1936).

Still, we humans all labor under implicit theories of knowledge, trying to match belief with that which is and discarding beliefs that systematically mislead. How might this work?

WITH NO GUARANTEES, IS REALISM STILL PLAUSIBLE?

A naturalist could travel broadly and see several thousand swans. Suppose all the swans he has seen are white. He might conclude that he now knows that "All swans are white." But does he? The observation of a single black swan disqualifies the naturalist's claim that "All swans are white" as an instance of knowledge, and how can he know that he has seen all of the swans? Perhaps he has not been to Australia and thus has not encountered any of the black swans that live there. There seems to be a legitimate worry here. If there is *no absolute guarantee* of true belief, how can people legitimately claim to have some beliefs that constitute knowledge?

Again, the ancients were already sensitive to this problem. There emerged a school of thought still with us today that is known as skepticism (Unger, 2002). The skeptics concluded that there is no point at which the "How do you know?" question is rendered null and void. At any point in an investigation, one can always ask "How do you know?" Even Socrates's "Know thyself" does not skirt the skeptic's worry. As any clinical psychologist will attest, people are deceived about themselves quite often.

The skeptic's challenge is indeed worrisome. Yet the challenge itself appears to lead to a paradox, because it seems to lead to the conclusion that nothing can be known. All knowledge claims, like all other beliefs, are relative to individuals holding them, and they are therefore mere historical accidents of culture. This is because truly human observations and thinking processes are inherently fallible. Ah, but if the skeptic *knows* this, then what? Then knowledge exists! On the other hand, if the skeptic *does not know* this, then what happens to the skeptic's challenge?

One response is to allow that absolute truth can never be assured. Those who seek knowledge should focus on evidence and warranted levels of confidence, rather than on the metaphysics of absolute, true belief (Chisolm, 1982; Plantinga, 1993). Knowledge is about criteria for favoring a class of beliefs as superior, differentiating them from the entire class of all possible beliefs.

But, hold on! There *do* seem to be proofs of some beliefs. As far back as Pythagoras and Euclid, plane geometry seemed certain. Pythagoras demonstrated that every triangle has angles totaling 180 degrees. Euclid asserted that if you take any line on a plane and a point not on that line, one and only one line can be drawn through the point parallel to the line. Take a sheet of paper and draw all the triangles or lines with a point not on a given line and you will find these claims seem true in all imaginable cases. Is this certainty at last?

There is a certainty here, but only in the context of geometry done on a plane. Draw a triangle on the outside of a ball and one on the inside as well. The one on the outside will always have greater than 180 degrees and the one on the inside always have less than 180 degrees. And there is more.

Imagine your line not on a plane but drifting indefinitely in space of three dimensions or more. There may be an infinite number of lines that can be drawn through a point not on the line and yet parallel to it! The truths of plane geometry are compelling when restricted to the world of two dimensions. But loosen the restrictions and look beyond a plane, and the search for Grand Truth again becomes unbridled.

If you find all this frustrating and confusing, you are not alone. Great minds for over two millennia still wrestle with these problems. So, are these problems a waste of time?

Not in the least! We need criteria to evaluate what we think we know simply in order to survive. Is that mushroom safe to eat, or is it deadly? How do you best evaluate such claims when people give you their answers?

What deductions for business meals can I get under this year's tax code? Is there a genetic cause for a particular ailment? Is it wrong to lie? Sometimes? Always? Is the world as it now exists in peril from accelerating global warming? Answers to each of these question matter. Because they matter, how the answers are to be evaluated as claims to knowledge matters a great deal.

CAN SOCIALLY CONSTRUCTED PICTURES GIVE US SOMETHING LIKE TRUTH?

The pressure to best evaluate what answers to inquiry should count as knowledge, given the ever-present challenge of skepticism, has led some to opt for something called **social constructionism** as a response to these concerns (Berger & Luckmann, 1966).

The work of the physicist and historian of science Thomas Kuhn is generally credited as having inspired the development of social constructionism. Have you ever heard the term *paradigm shift*? You can probably thank Thomas Kuhn for that. His *The Structure of Scientific Revolutions* (1970, 2nd ed.) is the only book to ever be cited more often than the Bible in a single decade. Here are some of the provocative things that Kuhn wrote in his account of the changes in the ways particular fields of science understand the world: "As in political revolutions, so in paradigm choice—there is no standard higher than the assent of the relevant community" (p. 94). And later, after describing how competing paradigms are "incommensurable"—that is, they have no common measuring stick to compare them with—Kuhn writes that

> the proponents of competing paradigms practice their trades in two different worlds. . . . Just because it is a transition between incommensurables, the transition between competing paradigms cannot be made a step at a time, forced by logic and neutral experience. (Kuhn, 1970, p. 150)

And this statement sums it up: "The transfer of allegiance from paradigm to paradigm is a conversion experience that cannot be forced" (p. 151).

Many postmodern scholars take Kuhn's descriptions of paradigm shifts as evidence that Kuhn thought the world of Newton was different from the world of Aristotle, and that Newton's world was in turn different from the world of Einstein. Social construction asserts that, since we can never know what is true, we should settle for how things appear to some at a given moment of time. Truth is out the window in the social constructionist view. Felicitous collaboration among a community of stakeholders is put in its place.

In the 1990s, physicist Alan Sokal all but destroyed variants of this view. In a move that came to be called the "Sokal hoax," he created a fake theory of physics using big words and convoluted sentence structures. He then got the nonsense published in a major postmodern journal. After the piece was published, he wrote an article telling the world how he pranked the journal editors. His point was that simple social agreement will never reveal much of reality (Sokal & Bricmont, 1999).

Less dramatic, but perhaps more profound, is Kuhn's own position that he explained in a conversation with Paul Wagner. After Kuhn had published a very dense historical account of black-body radiation and its study by scientists (Kuhn, 1987), Wagner asked Kuhn to join him for lunch at a place in

Harvard Square. Being a bit of a nerd groupie, Wagner brought along a copy of Kuhn's book and asked him to sign it. Kuhn wrote, "Tell the world this is my best book." Wagner asked, "Why this book and not *Structure*?"

Kuhn responded that he never intended people to take *Structure* as seriously as they did. *The Structure of Scientific Revolutions* began as a series of lecture notes for non-science undergraduate majors. It was intended as a sketch to show some of the human side of science, but it definitely was not intended to argue that science is only a human social phenomenon and nothing more.

Social constructionism is a type of relativism. "I am no relativist," Kuhn explained. "I am a physicist. Of course I believe there is a world out there, independent of our social agreements and regardless of what physicists say about it at different times. I wrote this *Black-Body Theory* book so people could see that this is what I believe and hope they will interpret *Structure* differently."

Kuhn's realism is not extreme. He is a realist, but he is not a correspondence theorist who insists that knowledge and truth must be considered as one. For Kuhn, as for many realists, knowledge sums up truth-seeking activities that aim to represent reality as closely as possible. Communities of scholars, including physicists, may see and talk about the world differently in response to social and other contextual cues, but that doesn't mean they live in different worlds or that the world itself is changing in response to human thinking about the world. Humans have the power to change the world, but not just by sharing their thinking about it. Kuhn's note in the *Black-Body Theory* book and his explanation are profoundly revelatory. There is a reality that knowledge aims to represent. When it succeeds, that is called truth.

IF NOT SOCIAL AGREEMENT, THEN WHAT?

Figuring out ways to evaluate better claims to know is a daunting task. Still, it cannot be laid aside as simply a matter of how this or that group tends to talk about things. Just as humans scour the world for greater evidence to support this or that belief, so too humans continue to anguish over—productively at times— how to evaluate claims to know this or that. But truth cannot be the criterion by which a claim to know is justified. Truth, as Kuhn alludes, is the ideal that knowers seek, but truth is not itself the product of truth-seeking. When done well, truth-seeking leads to knowledge, not to truth itself in any grand sense.

Truth-seeking is the mission of those who wish to know. For most realists, knowledge is not the acquisition of truth—certainly not Grand Truth. Knowledge is comprised of the best approximation of the truth that avoids evident error (Sosa, 2015). Knowledge is achieved with increasingly plausible explanations of what is even if, as C. S. Peirce warns, we can never achieve the ideal for which we aim (Ayer, 1968).

Perhaps in rather short order the reader can see that constructing a sustainable theory of knowledge is a Herculean intellectual task! It is no wonder that work on the theory of knowledge continues unabated, much as work in physics and other sciences seems never to be complete. In getting closer to truth, what can we trust in mastering a reliable process? Can we trust the information delivered by our senses? Can we trust reason?

Social constructionists, other relativists and, even more so, extreme skeptics, relentlessly push the "How do you know?" question until there seems nothing left to stand on save shifting sands of perspective and cultural conventions for summing up impressions. Yet if that were the case, there would be no achievements of intellect.

GROUNDS FOR KNOWING WHAT'S REAL

In her award-winning book, *Achievement*, Gwen Bradford points out that knowledge of any type is always an achievement. For Bradford, knowledge of how to do something, or to know some propositional datum, is to deliberately fulfill a purpose that poses some difficulty. Bradford explains that knowledge always involves some success in reaching for mastery over one's surroundings (Bradford, 2015, p. 80). That achievement inevitably ties perception and ratiocination together. Let's first consider perception.

Tyler Burge points out that if there was not a great deal of **intersubjective agreement** among humans regarding the appearances of the world, humans would have gone extinct (Burge, 2010). Admittedly, one person's observation of teal may be another's perception of blue or green but, there is surely general agreement on distinguishing any of those sense impressions from impressions of, say, red, gold, white, and so on. The fact that there is such overlapping of sense impressions goes far in establishing generally reliable grounds for data collection.

Still, while it may be impossible to know when a bit of perceptual knowledge is unadulterated truth, humans have much in their sensory and cognitive resources that helps individuate impressions in largely shared fashion with other humans. In addition, we now know much about the neurological processing of patterns in brains to conclude that standard logic and causal inferencing are similar on a species-wide basis (Dehaene, 2014).

In short, there is much behind realisms' continued appeal to many—especially to most ordinary people leading ordinary lives. Unlike a narrow realism such as in correspondence theory, where knowledge must match representation to reality without error, a more generally conceived realism insists only on a reality existing beyond human mental states. Truth is the ideal that representative approximations aim for, and knowledge is recognized when the approximation seems optimal.

The theory of knowledge has spawned many "isms" competing for center court. As this is not a book for specialists, we summarily gather many "isms" together that share a central thesis. So, for the purpose of economy, the **correspondence theory of truth**, **internal realism**, and **foundationalism**, along with others, are gathered together as forms of realism. For example, in close sympathy with realists among the various theorists of knowledge are those called correspondence theorists. These thinkers insist that knowledge and truth must be identical. By this they mean that knowledge claims must correspond to actual states of existence in the world. The correspondence theorist's criterion for credibility sets a higher bar than most other realists demand. Instead, most realists are willing to work with the idea that knowledge is simply the best explanation of a world that genuinely exists.

There are subtle nuances that specialists point to as legitimating their unique take on knowledge of the world. Each are well-reasoned, but none can reasonably declare "game over." Hence, since this is simply an introduction to theory of knowledge as implicitly held by the broadest set of stakeholders in education, we set aside details in favor of sketching plausible scaffolding that can explain something of the mind-set of different stakeholders in education.

In broad outline, the various "isms" reflect the spirit of Kuhn's exasperated comment to Wagner, "Of course I am a realist, I am a physicist for gosh sakes." Whether one is a scientist or layperson, all realists agree that there is an external world about which much can be known. Realists have an ideal most can agree upon, namely, that there is a world beyond human imagination and that the world can be represented in some shareable fashion. Realists recognize the acquisition of knowledge as an achievement. Realists encourage unrelenting truth-seeking. Realists welcome well-meaning challenges to knowledge claims. Realists build arguments and explanations in lieu of mere opinionated claims to know.

The dream for the realist remains as it was for Socrates, Plato, and Aristotle: to say of what is, that it is, and to say of what is not, that it is not. This is truly foundational for those at this most broad level of stakeholders in education.

IF REALISTS ARE ALL THAT, WHY ARE THERE SKEPTICS STILL?

Let's be clear here. Truth is an ideal for the realist. Commitment to a world beyond human conjuring is taken as a given. But because truth is an ideal, any one claiming to be a truth-seeker must naturally nurture skepticism in one self and in others.

Not just any representation will do for the realist. The representation must capture reality—the way things in fact are—as fully and accurately as possible. The only way to know if the representation succeeds is to subject it to a variety of evaluations. These range from experimental testing, review of logical organization, and the scaffolding of explanations purporting to be the best to date. Withstanding critical evaluation certifies only the representation's credibility in the search for truth.

All genuine truth-seekers must be skeptical to an extent. But radical skeptics disallow constructive talk about approaching truth. For the skeptic, the search for knowledge turns inevitably into something of a nightmare. The skeptic's nightmare is all the worse for the fact that, wherever he turns, the chance to embrace a tool for sorting through the world's apparent presentations is elusive.

On the one hand the skeptic knows, or *seems to know*, that every knowledge claim can be hammered into dust with the persistent use of the "How do you know?" question. With nothing to finally settle the matter of "How do you know?" in any specific case, it seems as if nothing can be known. This surely is a bleak and nightmarish conclusion for anyone who sets out to understand life and its surroundings. And yet things can get even worse for the skeptic.

Radical skeptics finding no grounds on which to base any claim to know, and find themselves claiming rather oddly that nothing can be known. Thus, when the skeptic makes the claim that nothing can be known, he is making a claim to know! The very thing he said was impossible to do!

Some skeptics like Peter Unger (2002) have invented ingenious ways to try to circumvent this apparently paradoxical position, but neither he nor any other skeptic seems to have succeeded in the eyes of most other epistemologists. For a helpful survey, see the entry "Epistemology" in *The Stanford Encyclopedia of Philosophy* by Mattias Steup and Ram Neta (2020).

Radical skeptics typically press their case by arguing that the knowledge claims of realists and others depend on having the truth in hand. That, in fact, is not required in many realist positions. This is where most skeptical arguments fall flat. Again, truth is an ideal. Knowledge is an achievement. But knowledge is not an achievement that involves grasping pure and unadulterated truth.

Despite its nightmarish results as a theory of knowledge, skepticism is far from dead. And that is probably a good thing! On the one hand, skepticism offers little hope for understanding oneself and one's environment. However, on the other hand, we cannot lay aside strategic skepticism altogether. Strategic skepticism illuminates error and directs truth-seekers away from it.

Doubt is what rescues people from intellectual complacency. Doubt shakes loose the rusted hinges of the doors of certainty. When these doors are loosened, then there is an opportunity to see through to new vistas of understanding. In short, truth-seekers themselves must think skeptically from time to time in productively strategic ways.

SUMMARY, RECOMMENDATIONS, AND CAVEATS

Summary

1. Truth exists. It contrasts with error and falsehood.
2. Truth is a community ideal and not simply an individual's mental event.
3. As an ideal, truth stands in contrast to important, but nonetheless misleading, worldviews that allow "my truth versus your truth."
4. There is a world "out there," which is beyond the turbulence of individual minds and which may be effectively represented and then shared.
5. Successful truth-seeking results in knowledge that leads away from error.
6. The further people move away from error, the closer they approach truth.

7. Genuine truth-seekers treasure doubt as a principle means of invigorating the search for truth within the Great Conversation of Humankind.

Recommendations

1. Treat the search for truth as a community ideal by encouraging everyone to step forward to support increasingly resilient knowledge claims.
2. Be bold in seeking knowledge that is free of evident error. But remain modest when making knowledge claims, because truth can rarely be grasped wholly and securely.
3. Always be prepared to doubt beliefs—even those privileged beliefs a person or community count as knowledge. Doubt rescues us from intellectual complacency.
4. There is never sufficient reason to settle for radical relativism for all matters deserving of considered judgment.
5. Treat truth-seeking as a moral duty imposed by any search for knowledge.
6. Avoid intellectual complacency at all costs by keeping a mind appreciative of sound justification open to the need for revision from time to time.

Caveats

1. Remember, truth is an ideal. It is something to reach for. It is rarely if ever something to be grasped once and for all.
2. Moving closer to truth does not guarantee that a dramatically different approach will appear to lead away from current knowledge claims to even better approximations of truth.
3. Intellectual complacency suffocates interest in looking beyond what persons or cultures currently believe.

Chapter Two

Why Children and Their Parents Are Natural Realists

IS THERE A REALITY, AND
DO STUDENTS NATURALLY KNOW IT?

Students, especially younger ones, want to learn the world's truths. Evolutionary psychologists and neuroscientists have demonstrated that learning is instinctual for humans at every age (Dehaene, 2014). Tyler Burge explains that the species would have vanished long ago if humans were not able to share agreement about the immediate world. This fits with the realist theory of knowledge discussed in the previous chapter (Burge, 2010). Furthermore, teachers take satisfaction in sharing truth with students. In short, truth seems to be central to how most stakeholders see the purpose of education. Yet, too little is said about the relationship between truth and the knowledge delivered to learners. It is knowledge humans acquire, not truth—at least not in any certain sense. So, how do stakeholders know when students in fact know more about the world?

To know that learners know more about the world, serious attention must be given to the idea of what it means to *know that one knows*. A theory of knowledge is not the same as a theory of truth. A theory of truth is a metaphysical challenge, while a theory of knowledge has more modest ambitions. As explained in the previous chapter, truth can serve as an important ideal for stakeholders in education, but that still leaves open the task of determining when learners have successfully acquired knowledge available for understanding.

Understanding is mastery of knowledge. But there can be no understanding in the absence of knowing what it is to know. Consequently, the theory of knowledge is the ground zero of the educational enterprise. Thus, before we can conclude that teachers are teaching well or students are learning well, we must agree on a theory of knowledge from which criteria of accountability can be derived.

There can be no accountability about teaching and learning without a theory of knowledge. The theory of knowledge establishes how and why an acquired set of beliefs or acquired skills should be privileged above competing sets of beliefs and skills. This is not a straightforward matter. The previous chapter sketched out what stakeholders at this foundation level implicitly seek when attempting to fulfill their shared sense of purpose in education—namely, to identify *properly privileged* beliefs.

WHERE DO WE START?

In Plato's dialogue *Meno*, Socrates seems to show that, because Meno's slave boy could construct a geometric justification for a problem set before him, the boy *knew* geometry, all without any previous instruction (Plato, 2002). Compare this with what one often finds when using multiple-choice test items in schools today. It is assumed that, if the student recognizes the best answer from a grouping of four or five choices, then the student *knows* the answer.

Plato, evidently like many psychometricians today, is willing to take a student's behavior of *pointing to* an option as evidence that the student recognizes and hence truly knows how to address an intellectual query. But surely there is more to knowing a properly privileged belief or skill than simply pointing to a conventionally accepted answer.

In the case of multiple-choice items, many factors may lead to pointing to a test designer's favored answer. Ideally, the behavior issues forth from the student's knowledge, but that is not always the case. Students may point to a test-maker's favored answer without knowing much of anything. For example, the students may vaguely recognize an option as simply more familiar than others. More often than not, that may work, but should that count as knowledge? And, if there is no knowledge, then neither is there understanding.

From the time of Meno's slave boy to contemporary test preparation today, cynics note that students can be led or "coached" with the result of increasing their chances of exhibiting favored behavior while remaining in near-total ignorance of the subject. And of course, a multiple-choice test with four options per test item rewards wholly ignorant guesses as "correct" 25 percent of the time. Surely this is not evidence of knowledge!

And, even if the student learned the correct answer to a stem, what exactly should that mean to anyone? Is that knowledge, or is it the outcome of deft psychologizing of test designers? Teachers, textbooks, and test makers can be wrong. A student responding on cue is evidence of being well-trained, perhaps, but, it surely cannot be sufficient evidence that the student knows something. What if the teacher and the sources of knowledge are themselves wrong? Simply ignorantly agreeing with the ignorant trainers does not make a student response an indication of knowledge. In short, a "correct" test answer could be demonstrable evidence of ignorance!

The requirements of knowledge must be made of sterner stuff than simply correct answers on multiple-choice tests. Knowledge must ground understanding. Then, understanding may lead to further well-grounded knowledge. Education should be about invigorating mental life and not merely shaping habitual shifts in behavioral propensities. Multiple-choice tests are merely a relatively inexpensive way to scan for behaviors resulting from certain types of training such as "drill and grill" and instructor coaching. Consequently, multiple-choice items quantify behaviors that, at times, may at best be only be indirectly related to the acquisition of knowledge.

Stakeholders at the ground level of educational practice—teachers, parents, employers, fellow citizens, and students themselves—share a commonsense intuition that education should be about learning to distinguish between (1) true, false, and indeterminate; between (2) right, wrong and indeterminate; and between (3) beliefs based on knowledge versus mere beliefs, opinions, suspicions, and all sorts of other mental events. In short, stakeholders at this level intuitively and generally believe there is an important relationship between truth, reality, and knowledge.

A WORLD OF THE SENSES: CONFIRMATIONS AND DISCONFIRMATIONS

Developmental psychologist Jean Piaget and the logician E. W. Beth together discussed the evidence for determining when a student can be said to have truly learned something (Piaget, 1954; Beth & Piaget, 1974). Each agreed that students having learned something was an achievement in the acquisition of knowledge. Piaget favored perceptual and neurological development as evidence of knowledge acquisition, whereas Beth favored the mastery of a justifying argument as key to demonstrating the acquisition of knowledge.

Neither saw knowledge as simply a contextually defined instance of behavior such as selecting the correct response to a multiple-choice item. In fact, save for a few lingering behaviorists, few learning theorists today reduce knowledge acquisition to mere behavioral dispositions. Instead, knowledge is associated with some standard of justified belief.

To know that *one knows* is critical for understanding. And to know that one knows requires specific skills, dispositional judgement, emotional commitment, and background knowledge, all directed toward the evaluational claim that one knows that one knows. When students come to know that they know, their ability to exercise **autonomy** increases.

With every increase in personal autonomy, people are better able to take on the challenges of the world rather than be driven by the winds of transient social influence, whimsy, and capriciousness (Peters, 1966; Hirst, 1975). **Knowing that** one knows, coupled with **knowing how** one knows, largely fulfills what is typically meant by understanding

To understand that one knows something requires some ability in evaluating both the reasoning and evidence used to arrive at a conclusion. In this, Piaget and Beth were both right to an important extent. A parrot may say the right thing in context, but cannot explain why it is the right thing to say at the moment. Presumably education at its best leads ultimately to increased understanding of self and the surrounding world.

Certainly, this is likely the commonsense view of stakeholders at the foundational level of education. **Education** is largely about acquiring knowledge, and knowledge is wholly about those beliefs that are most likely true or are apt to lead to ever better approximations of truth. This is unavoidable commonsense intuition in this context, but it is not where we can rest easy for, as Timothy Williamson explains, in knowledge-seeking, "Common sense is the starting point and not the end point" (Williamson, 2018, p. 11).

School should be a place where students learn how to seek truth and evaluate knowledge claims. We describe this atmosphere elsewhere as constituting the Great Conversation of Humankind (Wagner et al., 2016, 2017, 2018). Admittedly schools do more than host the Great Conversation. *But hosting the Great Conversation is their central educational mission.*

Think about it. In the early grades, students come to school enamored with the idea that they are going to learn truths—many truths! Parents, too, think children are in school to learn truths both large and small. And, surely, teachers want to avoid teaching falsehoods, so they too are committed to the transmission of truths. It is not an overstatement to say that, at least in the early years of **schooling**, the theory of knowledge that dominates is some form of implicit realism.

As Tyler Burge explains, human survival depends on relatively reliable shared interpretations of responsiveness to the surrounding world (Burge, 2010). Wrong decisions can be irredeemable. The naturally imposed mandate to get things right is critical. Wrongful assessments, evaluations, and plans exact costs. This underscores that some minimalist realism is the most natural **default position** for a theory of knowledge.

Developmental, cognitive, and evolutionary psychologies all agree that humans do not come to the world with a blank slate. The human mind has evolved templates for arranging sensory input from the moment of birth, if not before. The patterns that the mind intuits are refined over time through both culture and education. Some patterns of information processing can become quite sophisticated in groupings of humans who specialize in various studies. But all depends initially on a mind that seeks to know that it knows (Sigmund, 2017; Wiley, 2015).

Culture and education add much, but evolution gave human thinking quite a head start when it comes to knowing practices (Tomasello, 2014). Think about it: the very word *representation* means that there is an identifiable something in mind that reliably aligns with that which is represented. Human brains are naturally representational. In addition, as psychologist Alison Gopnik notes, humans naturally order representations in a fashion meaningful for sharing (Gopnik, 2016).

Finally, any prudent ordering of representations must pass muster with some **counterfactual reflection**. Through counterfactual reflection, the mind can increase the accuracy of representation with whatever is encountered (Pearl & MacKenzie, 2018). Counterfactual reflection takes place when people look for the "what ifs" of the world. "That looks like a nice fellow approaching but *what if* he is not so nice? Then I should be on my guard. I must figure this out!"

Counterfactual reflection constitutes much of human imagination, and it plays a key role in evaluating the strength and relevancy of evidence. "Maybe if the batter faced a different direction, his hit would not have broken a window. What if we move the ball field around? Would that make a difference?"

Furthermore, in the speculative creation of hypotheses, reasoning skills and counterfactual reflection may be augmented by fantasies that lead the mind to explore further possibilities of approximately true and false, of nearly right and wrong. This type of reasoning is called *abduction* (Williamson, 2018). Counterfactual reflection and abduction are tools properly utilized in all forms of realism.

Notice that theories of knowledge are not about creating knowledge itself. Rather, theories of knowledge are about evaluating the authority of claims to know (Piaget, 1954; Gopnik, 2016). By using available tools of evaluation, learners come to understand more of the credibility of specific claims to know. The ascent of knowledgeable evaluation is what leads to understanding.

Knowing in its most basic form is an orderly and structured reaction to presentations of what is beyond the brain. In short, people naturally expect that their accounts of how things are to fall into three categories: right (true), wrong (false), and cannot now be determined. From the earliest days of development and all through their learning lives, people are naturally inclined to divide what they think and experience into these three categories.

With this in mind, it is easy to understand why developmental psychologists such as Piaget and, more recently, Paul Bloom and Alison Gopnik, find studying children's ascent toward the more expert evaluation of evidence more illuminating than merely tracking behaviors of recognition in response to conditioned cues (Piaget, 1954; Bloom, 2005; Gopnik, 2016). Other animals learn to respond to stimuli, but humans alone evaluate how they know what they seem to know. The development of these evaluative practices is a critical step in extending student autonomy and mastery of the world they encounter. Acquisition of skillful evaluative practices is a learning achievement that separates humans from most, if not all, other mammals. All animals know many things, but what makes humans truly special is their widespread compulsion *to want to know how they know* that things are true.

In the early school years, children are often excited to learn many new things. Besides learning how to respond in successful ways to the world, such as caring for personal hygiene, tying shoes, and not making playmates mad, children want to learn that certain things are true. They learn facts such as turning up the thermostat will make the house warmer. Turning it down makes the house cooler. But knowing things of that sort soon gives way to stronger **epistemic** demands: "Mommy, why does turning the thermostat change the temperature in the house?" In other words, what *causes* the turning of a dial to lead to some subtle sounds and then warm or cool air coming in from specific places in each room? And parents should not be surprised when the day comes that the evidential basis of the previous explanation is questioned: "Daddy, how do you know that thermostats work the way you say?" The transition from mere acquisition of knowledge to a more genuine understanding reflects the learner's *implicit* awareness of theory of knowledge considerations. One may know some facts about thermostats, but cannot really understand them until one understands how they work.

The learner's desire to understand is too often shunted aside by parents and teachers alike. The desire to understand is frequently short-circuited by adults insisting that just pointing to the facts is all that is required for nearly any purpose at hand. Certainly, this is the message implied by extreme reliance on standardized tests to measure student intellectual growth. Besides stunting intellectual growth, pointing to this as the endpoint of knowing can entrench mistaken beliefs in students.

As children advance through school, they inevitably encounter mistaken beliefs. Mistaken beliefs may be innocently acquired as a result of relying on standard sources of information in their world. Intellectual development requires nurturing participation in the Great Conversation of Humankind, in which a *shared understanding* of what is presumed to be known is strongly sought by all.

RELATIVISTIC SHAPING

Knowing that one knows is an achievement, an excellence for which there is no substitute. But if the learning environment discredits such excellence and substitutes something as good enough instead, the search for excellence may dissipate. The ideal of searching for truth requires a theory of knowledge focused on excellence in approximating truth. Acceptance of "good enough" in multiple-choice testing inherently ignores excellence of understanding.

Despite the suffocating effect of environments that substitute good enough responsiveness over the endless quest for excellence of understanding, some astute students recognize errors in what they were taught. They also recognize that much of what they were taught rests on little more than source authority. Reasons for positive evaluation and conviction seem all but absent. Some things, they decide, need to be questioned. Not only do such suspicions arise naturally in astute students, but teachers themselves often deliberately encourage students in these suspicions in an effort to teach critical thinking.

As a result, students often find themselves faced with teachers, news outlets, peers, and many others prompting doubt in matters that they previously thought resolved, given favorable scores on various multiple-choice tests. What to do? Whom to believe? Where to go to find decent information? Does it even matter whether we get things right or wrong—maybe it is all just relative to moment and context? What if there is no truth to pursue, only answers that make someone in power happy?

Prompting doubts in students is often a good thing. After all, doubt is what rescues students from a life of intellectual complacency (Wagner et al., 2018). But unbridled doubt can quickly descend into an impoverished skepticism where the ideal of truth is discredited. If students are not yet sufficiently sophisticated to understand truth as an ideal, what will happen? If students are discouraged from seeing that earnest truth-seeking reveals important questions and furthers understanding, what will happen?

These students may lapse into radical skepticism or, worse, **moral nihilism**. They deserve better than that. They deserve to see that, while truth is necessarily elusive, greater understanding of many matters is genuinely possible. After all, books, buildings, professions, transportation systems, complex algorithms in computer science, and much more did not arise by error or happenstance.

While well-placed skepticism develops the evaluative skills central to becoming critical thinkers, poorly placed radical skepticism simply makes people into negative, pessimistic thinkers. Timothy Williamson writes, "If you are really unwilling to make assumptions your conversation partners won't grant, you hand them terrifying power over your own thought. Skeptics will . . . exploit that power to drag you into the skeptical pit with them" (Williamson, 2018, p. 34).

Evolutionary psychologists make it clear that people have a natural learning instinct. Whether it is children exploring a playground, astronauts exploring Mars, or accountants reviewing a balance sheet, each is trying to figure out what is true or false, right or wrong in their area of investigation. Trial-and-error responsiveness guides much of this learning.

And the human learning instinct drives us beyond the world of immediate sensory perception. Human learning leads to conjuring abstract concepts of infinity, morality, the supernatural, and more. Elsewhere we describe these propensities collectively as the **Law of Figuring Things Out** (Wagner et al., 2018).

Figuring things out comes naturally to people, who employ disparate sets of algorithms for making new inroads into the unknown (Davies, 2019). They typically share their conclusions so that they can be evaluated by others. When students profess to dislike school, their complaint is often directed at school processes rather than any experience with the Great Conversation. Schooling may compromise the propensity of students for figuring things out by ignoring the theory of knowledge and its evaluational **commitments**, **dispositions**, and **skills**, opting instead for teaching to the test.

The default position of the conscious human brain is to learn! One can learn truths as easily as one can learn falsehoods, but the natural default position focuses not on learning by itself but on learning *likely truths*. And this latter learning involves knowing that you know. Have you ever watched someone eating a bowl of cereal alone in a room? They may listen to the radio, watch television, or read a book or a newspaper. Take all that away and most will read the back of the cereal box. Humans' natural state is to want to learn, to want to know more. In most cases, they want to know that they know more. Realism is the expectation that, for what one knows, one has good reason to claim to know it. By contrast, radical skepticism and relativism just will not satisfy humans' natural learning instincts.

If teachers are not teaching students "the truth," then students and their parents have reason to ask, "So, what is the purpose of students going to school?"! One cannot get far in constructing a defense for educational institutions without addressing the concept of knowledge and the ideal of truth.

TRUTHING AND LYING

Imagine a teacher teaching students things she herself does not know to be true. Maybe she does not have much evidence to support her conclusions and cannot respond to student questions such as "How do we know that is true?" Perhaps the teacher does not believe the truth of what she is teaching, so again she is teaching what she does not know. How can that be right? What are other stakeholders at this level of education to think about such teaching?

Teachers want to teach things that are true and not false, right and not wrong. Students want to learn what is true, not merely convenient falsehoods. Parents want to know their children are learning truth and not mere opinions or standardized lies. Most stakeholders at this level see truth as the alpha and omega of proper educational practice. They expect institutional commitment to conveying the truth as best as possible.

A teacher adds a sum incorrectly and the children laugh. She got it wrong. She is not supposed to do that. A teacher makes a snide remark about conservatives or progressives. Students whose parents are one or the other may take offence and suspect the teacher is dishonoring her professional commitment to trade only in truth. Students correct their parents' dating of the August 28, 1968 riots at the Democratic Convention in Chicago, and they take pride in having learned the truth about something their parents got wrong. Truth addiction!

To appreciate how unique truth is, all we have to do is to look to our language. Our language regards truth as unique. Mental events all have both noun and verb forms. Truth does not. Mental events include things such as: thinking and thoughts, doubting and doubts, believing and beliefs, suspecting and suspicions, care and caring, lie and lying—but there is no truthing. This is because truth is not a mental event. Mental events happen in heads. Truth is outside any individual human mind or any collective. Truth is a representation of what is without error. There is truth as a noun, but no verb form of its happening. Truth just is a special relationship between a thing and exactly that same thing represented.

Everything centers around expectations in truth-seeking practices. The Law of Figuring Things Out says truth-seeking practices involve such diverse actions as evaluating the adding of sums, being cautious about accepting snide political remarks, and recognizing legitimate authority when evaluating someone's claim to know. In the paragraph above, all of these evaluative practices are exemplars of what matters in a truth-centered activity where genuine "figuring things out" is happening.

As children mature, they often find that the search for truth becomes a search for a palpably more elusive quarry. Some truth claims that they entertained in the past turned out to be wrong. They were fooled. They begin to note that even respected adults sometimes get things wrong. And, worse, evolution equipped every species of prey with some skills of deceit. This means that people lie, that is, people of all ages may lie at times. Yet, truth matters. But how?

Students need to learn that some claims should be taken with a grain of salt. Other claims need to be taken more seriously. But how do you learn to tell the difference between the two? Teachers, under a misguided notion of critical thinking, may encourage students to be distrustful of *all* truth claims—especially those of authorities. Does this help them to honor the realist commitment that truth matters?

Implicit in any realist approach to the theory of knowledge is the expectation that knowledge claims are best authorized when they muster evidence and argument to avoid foreseeable error. Truth is explicitly on the radar of any realist. Realists are truth-seekers. This seeking drives their evaluative demands on knowledge claims made by themselves or others. Truth is the realist ideal. Knowledge is the realist achievement. Yet many older students in high school and college seem to worry that, if the ideal of truth cannot be realized, then skepticism is inevitable. Too often they fail to realize that if they push this reasoning further, they fall into contradiction because simple skepticism says "we cannot know anything"—but then acts as if this sweeping denial of knowledge is somehow *known* to be true. Students need to learn that modesty of ambition is appropriate, that humans' knowing vulnerabilities need to be accepted, all the while keeping a firm grasp on the ideal of knowledge building.

Lies, biases, and our observational frailties all seem to count against the idea that truth-seeking can be a sustainable goal for education. But there is no need to lapse into despair at this point—not just yet!

In the theory of knowledge of most students, parents, and teachers, truth-seeking is the ideal that justifies educational institutions. Whether or not this ideal should be held is not the issue here; rather, truth matters a great deal to the overwhelming majority of stakeholders at this level of educational practice. To serve stakeholder interests, realism must drive many curricular decisions and instructional strategies.

MEANINGFUL AND REAL

Ideals are not always realized in manifest achievements. Ideals, in their simplest and most robust form, identify that which is valued, that which deserves to be worked for. Acquiring accurate knowledge and knowing the strength of the knowledge claim is always an achievement. In contrast, mere learning may not be an achievement at all in some cases (Bradford, 2015), but even without the philosophical insight of Gwen Bradford, the stakeholders discussed in this chapter converge on the idea that knowledge is an achievement.

Students can learn that certain foods upset their stomachs without giving much thought to the matter. In contrast, no one secures genuine knowledge without subjecting the information acquired to some critical review. Subsequently, the knowledge acquired must be *meaningful*, that is, the knowledge can be deployed as needed by an understanding knower.

Realism dictates that knowledge claims can be right or wrong. Whether it is Gertrude Stein's "A rose is a rose is a rose" or President Obama's claim that "You can put lipstick on a pig but it is still a pig," the message is that things are what they are and nothing else. People generally endorse this straightforward view, but that does not commit them to a theory of knowledge that says that there is knowledge only when there is a full and complete match between a representation and a piece of reality.

Remember that truth, not knowledge, is the ideal of realist truth-seeking efforts. Knowledge, by contrast, is comprised of claims that most plausibly account for the available evidence. To have knowledge, evidence must be processed using the standard rules of inference for that sort of inquiry in order to move credibly from the evidence to the most plausible conclusion. The theory of knowledge is about evaluating evidence and constructing and evaluating the best way of processing that evidence to grasp more about reality. The Law of Figuring Things Out leads us to seek the ideal that truth represents. Knowledge is the product that most closely approximates reality when compared to competing beliefs and opinions. Knowledge is what best helps us get things done. In short, we do better when we know what we are doing.

Truth is the ideal that education seeks. Knowledge, as in meaningful understanding of what is real, is the highest achievement of education. However, the ambition to know the truth can be frustrated. Lies, mistakes, and clumsy thinking all lead away from the most plausible account of how things are. Ambition thwarted often enough can lead to abandonment of truth-seeking and the despair of total skepticism or **nihilism**. Furthermore, abandoning the search for truth can often lead people to a sense of meaninglessness.

By contrast, lives centered around truth-seeking are meaningful in many ways. The search for truth depends on a *shared* reliance on our evolved representational systems. Truth-seeking is inherently cooperative, even if this cooperation is indirect at times. In addition, genuine truth-seeking involves seeking criticism from others about where and how our efforts may have gone wrong. As a result, schemes for structuring evidence and evaluating it are shared and are continually evolving in any learning community.

These meaning-making properties require truth-seeking to be communal, strategic, and fostered by relentless commitment to sharing with others. We have described this vision of education elsewhere as participation in the Great Conversation of Humankind. We make meaning together by bringing all stakeholders in this level of education into the Great Conversation of Humankind.

In contrast, lives lose meaning if they are lured into radical skepticism. Radical skepticism leads to conversations in which polemic and dominant personalities rule. The meaningful gives way to the arbitrary, the capricious, and the destructively idiosyncratic.

Socrates, giving a bit of self-help advice, once famously challenged: "Know thyself." But skepticism says: "Forget about it! Nothing can be known!" As a result, instead of meaningful engagement with others, skepticism promotes a bleak sense of meaninglessness and despair. Teachers can aim to make their classrooms *sanctuaries of meaningfulness*. Every teacher should honor her classroom as a doorway to the Great Conversation. Since students naturally want to be freed from prior misconceptions, they are by nature truth-seekers and can be open to participating in the Great Conversation.

ODE TO CURIOSITY AND INTELLECTUAL ADVENTURE

To fulfill this aim, classrooms should honor great truth-seekers past and present. Nobel Laureates and Fields Medalists honored for their achievements in mathematics should be visible in each classroom as relevant to the lived world. Even more important, teachers should take on the challenge of sending children home each day with one good question to ponder. Treasure the question! This makes it plain that the Great Conversation lives through truth-seeking and not mere answer-giving.

The Great Conversation has characteristic features. These include dispositions, skills, **virtues**, and a relentless truth-seeking commitment. Most important, perhaps, is that the Conversation *explicitly* adopts truth as an ideal. The Conversation's quest for knowledge is an approach to that ideal. The goal is always to move away from the wrong and the false and towards the right and the correct, as much as our available resources allow.

Not every classroom practice honors these expectations. For example, in science education it is easy to demonstrate the credibility of Robert Hooke's law that doubling the weight at the end of a spring will double the length of the spring's extension. In mathematics, it is easy to demonstrate that the addition of any number greater than zero to another number greater than zero leads to a larger number than either number alone. But establishing credibility in some subjects is inherently more difficult than in others.

Think about a class in literature. What is the "truth" in Hermann Hesse's *Siddhartha*, William Golding's *Lord of the Flies*, George Orwell's *1984*, or, Aldous Huxley's *Brave New World*? As every student knows, Cliffs Notes give reliably general answers to standardized test items about these books. But what are the truths depicted in these books, or in the poems of Sylvia Plath or Elizabeth Barrett Browning? What are the truths in literature?

One of the authors informally polled a group of medical doctors about the six most important books they remember reading in high school. *Siddhartha*, *Lord of the Flies*, *1984*, and *Brave New World* made everyone's list. If well-educated doctors can remember the importance of these books, that seems to speak well of their credibility. Yet, in what sense are these and other works of literature a credible source of knowledge beyond what is asked on a multiple-choice test?

The physicians queried were all specialists and in the twilight of their careers, many years beyond high school. Yet each independently listed these four stories as important learning from high school. In what way do you suppose such learning is "important" if not in some way extending human understanding of reality?

Discussion of these and other books certainly has a place in the truth-seeking function of the Great Conversation. But they do not lend themselves to the sort of directly demonstrable credibility one often finds in subjects such as science, math, logic, and other algorithm-driven subjects. Here it is important to remember that truth-seeking is an approachable ideal and no more, and that the appropriate manner of approaching truth will differ from discipline to discipline.

Nelson Goodman and Catherine Elgin argue that artists of all types know things (Goodman & Elgin, 1988). They argue that what artists know becomes evident when their intentions and perceptions are shared, at least to a degree, by attentive receivers of their artistic presentations. There is knowledge when the learners' understanding of the real is both shared and evident—and in this way, meaningful.

For example, those reading the passage in Leo Tolstoy's novel *Anna Karenina* in which Anna commits suicide are likely to feel closer to the experience of suicide than when they read any work of empirically based social science. This "feeling closer" is knowledge approximating the ideal of truth. The closer the artist brings others to the feel of the experience she is depicting, the more credible her exemplification of knowledge (Goodman, 1976).

THE PEDAGOGY OF MEANINGFUL UNDERSTANDING

Psychologist Albert Bandura and many others have gone to great lengths to explain the importance of role-modeling in student development (Bandura, 1976). Teachers can model participation in the Great Conversation of Humankind by engaging all students as if all were participating in it. Moreover, teachers can role-model what it means to honor the truth-seeking enterprise by showing their own unabashed esteem for masters in truth-seeking engagements.

Good teachers know to draw attention to master truth-seekers. For example, art teachers often feature award-winning champions on bulletin boards. In literature, there are Nobel Prize winners and there are Pulitzer Prize and many other "Book of the Year" award winners. There are awards in all the arts and sciences for excellence in achievement. Of course, the champions in a field are not always recognized in timely fashion with an award, but over time they can be identified by the recognition that accrues to their work. Understanding, whether in the arts or sciences, is necessarily meaningful. Understanding extends personal recognition of one's place in the world and how one can navigate the world more readily.

Admittedly, in the social studies the problem of including seminal figures may be more challenging. For example, is it more important to talk about what Martin Luther King, Jr. said or what he did? Both, you might say. Ah yes, but is that always the case? What about dissenting voices in cultural history in times past and present? Should Steve Bannon and Che Guevara be given equal time or equal treatment in a curriculum? How should the social impact of the Scopes "monkey trial" be discussed?

The commitment to a theory of knowledge in the rest of the curriculum is shaken in the social studies. Skepticism and its derivatives seem more natural and can arise in unsettling fashion. Parents and the general public worry about whether what is taught in social studies is true or not! Their commitment to realism becomes palpable in their judgments and criticisms of public education. And there is more that is unsettling in the teaching of social studies.

Some teachers hoping to teach critical thinking ask students to look at diverse viewpoints and consider whose "truth" should win out—if any. Such relativism does little to anchor a sense of meaningful investigation on the part of students. Sometimes students learn only to be crassly cynical. These students regard truth as a fiction. They see all claims on equal footing, that is, all equally incorrect as approximations of knowledge. For some, truth becomes nothing more than a historical accident based on what an individual or group want to believe.

A commitment to relativism leads some students to conclude that "might makes right" when it comes to social matters. In this kind of environment, there is again little for the concerned student to "hang her hat on" when trying to figure things out. Meaninglessness and feelings of hopelessness contaminate the spirit of truth-seeking. In the end some students are prevented from further cooperative participation in the Great Conversation. If there is no right and wrong, no true or false, then what matters?

These are not inevitable consequences of teaching social studies, nor do they reflect the intentions of most well-meaning teachers. But in the effort to teach critical thinking, such things do at times occur and teachers must guard against them. Truth-seeking requires a degree of skepticism. After all, doubt is what rescues students from intellectual complacency. But doubt must not become either reckless or aired in a mean-spirited fashion if stakeholders are to seek shared understandings with one another.

Consider the case of Martin Luther King, Jr. He was both a historically significant leader and he was a moralist. He was an eloquent preacher, a Baptist, and yet he was a doubter in his youth who denied that Jesus rose from the dead. He meant his words to be taken seriously as right-minded and aligned with the will of God, but does he *know* what he is talking about? Do his words ring with plausible *truth-value*? Could his words be just one more set of opinions—no better and no worse than any other? Exactly how is a teacher who is committed to seeking and teaching the truth to present his life and witness to students?

Social studies teachers have a high hurdle to leap if they are to preserve the meaningfulness of the Great Conversation. "Sticking to the facts" sounds like a great rule of thumb, but facts do not speak for themselves. Facts, especially social facts, are always embedded in some story. Consider, for example, that both the public and the American Psychological Association (Peterson & Seligman, 2004) think there are some virtues that are right-minded. Do some of these virtues merit being taught in social studies, much as Hooke's Law is taught in physical science classes?

There are no two ways about it. In the theory of knowledge, truth matters when making knowledge claims to all the stakeholders at this level of educational practice. There must be a focus on distinguishing ideas, observations, and theories that better avoid error than those of competitors. The necessary focus for this effort to advance shared understanding is most transparent in a realist theory of knowledge. Remember that in this view, truth and knowledge, even though they are related, are not of one cloth. Truth is the ideal, a seamless match between a representation and a piece of reality. Knowledge is that select set of beliefs which optimally approximate truth without evident error. Education as the Great Conversation is about the search for truth, and knowledge is the product of that search. If teachers across the curriculum use strategies to focus attention on the acquisition of knowledge, plausible proposals and critical evaluations can robustly combine in a meaningful and shared search for accurate understanding of both the physical and the social world.

A realist theory of knowledge brings together what all stakeholders at this level strongly and reasonably expect from education at the classroom level. And, most importantly, within a realist theory of knowledge students have reason to believe that both what they are learning and what they hope to learn will add personal control and meaning in their lives.

Compare how the Russian psychologist Lev Vygotsky talks about a *zone of proximal development* (Vygotsky, 1978). He means that learners must share in sufficient background knowledge to make further investigation and learning fruitful. Before beginning further **didactic instruction**, teachers should take time to ascertain what students understand. Student understanding can only be appraised by getting them to talk about what they think they know they know. Standardized test scores therefore reveal little about students' increases in usable knowledge and capacity to figure things out. Recognizing the best selection on a multiple-choice exam hardly testifies to an increased capacity to figure things out (Koretz, 2017). But, as a stakeholder may reasonably ask, do test scores testify to teacher competency in any way?

One problem that increasingly has become a matter of concern is the use of numerical targets for holding teachers and educational leaders accountable, which all too often has led to only a mirage of objectivity. Sadly, schemes of manipulation and even outright cheating are inevitable when so much career security is at stake (Koretz, 2017; Deming, 2000; Campbell,

1975). Accountability summaries based on standardized tests do not provide knowledge of important student improvement such as the increased ability to figure things out.

Objectivity secured by multiple-choice test items is similarly a chimera when it comes to evaluating student learning. The standard definition of an objective test item is that it can be machine graded, but, as we will see later, that is no guarantee of anything worth calling objective in the answers. Machine-gradable test items cannot avoid having the subjectivity of designers make their way into questions, distractors, and answers. Hence the ideal of objectivity is at least partially an unavoidable illusion.

SUMMARY, RECOMMENDATIONS, AND CAVEATS

Summary

1. Students must learn that acquiring knowledge requires having shareable justifications that establish knowledge claims as closely approximating truth better than any competing claims.
2. Students want to learn truth. Students must be aware of how challenging the search for truth is without discouraging them from taking the quest seriously. Neither they nor their parents see the classroom as a place for simply supporting unsubstantiated opinions or regimenting behavior aimed at getting students past the next multiple-choice test.
3. Most teachers want to lead students away from evident error.
4. Neither parents nor students want students subjected to mere propagandizing, either through the curriculum or through inept teaching strategies.
5. In general, the public wants students to acquire intellectual resources that will make them independent adults one day, competent employees and professionals, informed citizens, good neighbors, and competent supporters of shared community. Education should build students capable of these competencies.

Recommendations

1. Teachers need to keep in mind and explain to students that no one, no thinking operation ever occurs without the benefit of assumptions. Not

even computers can think without explicit assumptions (Pearl & MacKenzie, 2018).
2. Truth-seeking cannot simply be taught. The tendency to seek truth is an inborn tendency, but it can be developed through watching it being role-modeled by others and through being engaged in truth-seeking with more experienced truth-seekers. Teachers lead students into appropriate truth-seeking practices by inviting them into the Great Conversation.
3. Standardized tests are unavoidable in today's highly regimented public schools. Still, teachers should minimize their use. Instead, students should be required to model their thinking and evaluative processes.
4. Teachers should create benchmarks for student building that demonstrate when students pass through thresholds of greater autonomous understanding (Wagner, 2018).
5. Teachers should make clear their own assumptions and those of both the curriculum and teaching strategies.
6. Teachers should imagine themselves as coaches teaching thinking skills from time to time. To do this, attention must focus on the two central questions of a theory of knowledge, namely: (1) How do you know____? and (2) What do you mean by your use of the term ____?
7. Teachers should never use classroom time to teach students how to scam multiple-choice tests so that students have no idea why certain answers are plausible but, instead, are simply demanded.

Caveats

1. Teachers who coach students on scamming multiple-choice tests are dishonoring education (Caplan, 2018: Koretz, 2017). This is a betrayal of every Level 1 stakeholder's commitment to a theory of knowledge.
2. Never sacrifice the ideal of truth to radical skepticism. To do so encourages students to be dismissive of the search for truth and consideration of the earnestly valued claims of others with whom they may disagree.
3. Never devalue learning by making it seem as nothing more than passing meaningless tests for some far-off authority.
4. Students need to know that education is *for them* and not for the careers of teachers, administrators, or politicians.

Chapter Three

Conceptions of Knowledge II

Contextualism and Pragmatism

THE DISORDERED IDEA OF PRAGMATISM

Pragmatism is known for declarations such as "inquirers should assess their beliefs or habits according to whether they lead to success" (Misak, 2016, pp. 222–223). This appeals to many people of action, who are on the go and who are in authority. It is unlikely the reader can even think of an administrator, policy-maker, or politician who does not claim to be a pragmatist. But what does pragmatism mean to these stakeholders?

If you ask them, they might boast, "I avoid abstractions. I am a problem-solver. I get to work on solving the problem at the moment." This shoot-from-the-hip response is amusing to those who have studied pragmatism. A hint as to why this response is so amusing becomes evident when these self-proclaimed pragmatists are asked how they know that they solved a problem.

Just because a problem seems to go away does not mean that the problem has been solved or that the problem-solver had much to do with actually solving it. Just because a problem goes away means only that it has *somehow* vanished! Indeed, there may not have been a real problem in the first place.

The vanishing of a problem may be due to factors unrelated to anything the problem-solver did. In addition, a problem may be solved for the moment but, perhaps, it could have been solved better and more permanently. Self-proclaimed problem-solvers seldom evaluate their actions in this light. The mere absence of distress seems sufficient to relieve their anxiety about a previously pressing problem. This is not the stuff of real pragmatism.

Authentic pragmatism is grounded in reflection on truth! Surprised? Pragmatism began as a theory of knowledge. It was never intended to be a metaphysical theory of truth. What does this mean?

Metaphysics is about ultimate reality. *If* it is possible for a representation to model reality meaningfully and without error, to correspond to reality as it truly is, *then* truth does indeed exist as a fundamental aspect of reality. This is the contention of **correspondence theorists** and many realists.

In contrast, the theory of knowledge, as opposed to metaphysical theories, is more modest in its conclusions. The theory of knowledge is about grasping truth as best one can, given a clear-eyed vision of human frailty in such matters. Pragmatists, as much as realists of various sorts, agree that truth exists. Pragmatists also agree with one another that truth cannot reliably be grasped with certainty (Misak, 2016, p. 286).

But pragmatism never doubts the existence of truth. In fact, it embraces the idea that truth exists and is foundational to what a pragmatic theory of knowledge can hope to achieve. Pragmatism focuses on identifying the most **plausible** claims for *approximating* truth or on the most apt resources for *aligning with* truth, given human frailty. Thus, pragmatism tries to accommodate the relation between truth and knowledge by arguing both that truth lies beyond the turbulence of human mental life and, further, that through optimally strategic methodologies, success in approximating truth is possible.

This pragmatic accommodation is usually achieved by acknowledging that truth exists, but then that acknowledgement is set aside in favor of strategic thinking for approaching the truth or, at least, avoiding the consequences of foreseeable error. Generally speaking, pragmatists focus on the theory of knowledge as a way to extend *successful human engagement with the world*. Pragmatists do not discard the idea of truth, but like William James (Misak, 2004), focus instead on engaging the world in an optimally satisfying fashion.

A pragmatic theory of knowledge can be thought of as a sort of *satisficing*, to borrow a term from economics. Satisficing is contrasted with seeking the absolutely best solution, and is about doing the best we can with available resources, about finding a solution that is "good enough." The saticficing approach of pragmatism aligns well with recent psychological research on how in fact adults normally evaluate situations (Ferreira et al., 2002; Ferreira et al., 2009). Note here that satisficing is a mental event, as Mikkel Gerken writes: "The Principle of Epistemic Satisficing postulates that the ubiquitous phenomenon of satisficing extends to the realm of epistemic judgment" (Gerken, 2017, p. 118).

Satisficing does not denote a relationship between what is represented and the representation, in contrast with the Tarskian definition of truth discussed in chapter 1. Rather, as Gerken explains, "Normally, an agent, A, forms epistemic judgments on the basis of a prima facie reason that is arrived at by processing only a limited part of the evidence that is available to A" (2017, p. 143). In short, satisficing is a strategy for minimizing risk of avoidable error.

Satisficing never confirms ideal results. Instead, it aims for results that minimize risk through avoidance of reasonably anticipated error. In the pragmatic theory of knowledge, the available resources are the human mind and sensory apparatus, cultural artefacts of cognition, and the manifest reality of the world (Ayer, 1968).

The challenge of pragmatism is constructing a theory of knowledge that aims for more than the vanishing of some local problem or challenge (Fantl & McGrath, 2002). It must be more systematic than what favorable happenstance might produce. For some pragmatists, such as William James, the systematic approach coordinates psychological comfort in the face of uncertainty (Misak, 2013). For other pragmatists, such as Charles Sanders Peirce, mere satisfaction is too often transient and illusory, and it can short-circuit deeper productive searches for more robust solutions (Misak, 2013). In short, there are variants of pragmatism as there are variants of realism.

ORIGINATING MOTIVATIONS OF PRAGMATISM AND THE HARVARD SCHOOL

By the close of the nineteenth century, there was an explosion of scientific insights. From Charles Darwin, George Boole, Michael Faraday, James Clerk Maxwell, and Augustus De Morgan to Ludwig Boltzmann, Heinrich Hertz, Henri Poincare, and Carl Gauss, biology, physics, logic, and mathematics leaped forward as never before.

To guide both science and well-reasoned common sense, a theory of knowledge was needed that prescribed strategies for avoiding needless errors and to advance reasoned hope for further understanding. Peirce was clearly the first whose unique depth and breadth of knowledge enabled him to sense what was needed for such a theory of knowledge (Peirce, 1868).

Pragmatism is sometimes said to be wholly American in origin. That is probably something of an overstatement. The earliest pragmatist, C. S. Peirce, was in frequent contact with Lady Welby and through her and others influenced F. P. Ramsey, Ludwig Wittgenstein, R. B. Braithwaite, and other British **instrumentalists** (Hardwick & Cook, 1977; Misak, 2008).

Peirce did indeed teach for a time at Harvard, as did fellow pragmatist William James. But John Dewey, the third founder of pragmatism after Peirce and James, did not. Dewey was trained at Johns Hopkins University and went from there to the University of Chicago and then to Columbia University.

By the end of the twentieth century there were five giants of pragmatic philosophy, four at Harvard. W. V. O. Quine is closely aligned with the thinking of Peirce, while Nelson Goodman and Hilary Putnam, both of Harvard, along with Richard Rorty of Princeton, are closely aligned with the thinking of James. Finally, Israel Scheffler, regarded by many as the dean of philosophy of education, was also at Harvard and is closely aligned with the thinking of John Dewey.

While those influential thinkers are deceased, pragmatism lives on, and arguably the most famous pragmatists today are Catherine Elgin of Harvard and Peter Achinstein, a Harvard graduate who teaches at Johns Hopkins University. Elgin is an intellectual descendant of Peirce, James, and Goodman (Elgin, 2017), and Achinstein (2019) acknowledges his indebtedness to Quine.

THE PIONEERS

Peirce was a competent mathematician who made original contributions to probability theory, linguistics, semiotics, and philosophy. Peirce noticed that when it came to figuring things out, humans have a special instinct for revealing hypotheses. He named this talent *abduction*, in contrast to deduction and induction. For Peirce, abduction delivered promising speculations about the nature of the world (Achinstein, 2019). Induction added credibility to hypotheses, and at times deduction could be employed as a tool for identifying testable hypotheses and for evaluating arguments (Misak, 2016).

Deductive arguments are truth-guaranteeing in light of their formal **validity**, but deduction cannot guarantee the soundness of arguments, their practical credibility. Soundness rests inevitably on observation and assumptions, properly arranged and weighted. This is a critical point insisted upon by all pragmatists.

Formal deductive reasoning looks very much like an algebraic equation. Given the truth of a set of premises, the conclusions of a valid deductive argument are guaranteed to be reliable. A sloppy attempt at a deductive argument is easy to spot and dispatch from serious consideration on grounds of being ill-formed. But when applying deductions to the world, where do the assumptions come from? Do people just make assumptions up? Sometimes. Do people acquire assumptions and other tentative conclusions from their previous experience with the world? Sometimes.

Peirce allowed that through the intuitive sensitivities of abduction, reasonable estimates of reality increase in credibility. Peirce recognized that there is a gap between what we can be reasonably sure of and what in fact might be true (Peirce, 1877). Probability assessment and abductively derived assessments, used wisely, give strength to inductively derived observations, but they do not guarantee T-R-U-T-H.

Evaluation of inductively derived information can be persuasive and lead researchers away from error. The path away from error is the path toward truth. Peirce believed strongly in the ideal and the reality of truth. But he doubted humans could ever know for sure that they, in fact, know the truth (Ayer, 1968). The vulnerabilities inherent in human knowing apparatus could never fully erase all possibility of error-laden inference.

With ever-increasing research skills and with the acquisition of additional information, Peirce believed it was undeniable that, over time, humans move ever farther away from error. Peirce, like the pragmatists who followed, recognized the need for criteria demarcating the most useful beliefs from less useful ones. Peirce recognized how probabilistic tools and practices of falsification often show when we can know we are wrong. Peirce's mathematical and scientific skills and dispositions continue to fit well with many of the evolving approaches to science over the past 30 years.

For example, software engineer David Auerbach, in his book *Bitwise*, quotes from Hans Reichenbach's book *Experience and Prediction*: "We do not see things, not even the concreta, as they are but in a distorted form: we see a substitute world—not the world as it is, objectively speaking." From this, Auerbach concludes, "This substitute world that we see is, in short, a lie. Our brains take sense data and inaccurately analogize it into forms that are already familiar to us" (Auerbach, 2018, pp. 15–16).

The world is there. Truth exists. But we see through a glass darkly. Our senses are like transducers that convert stimuli like sounds and light into various forms of neuronal activity. A proper theory of knowledge directs us to use our brains to best accommodate the **transducer caused disparity** between the world and our minds. We do what we can, deliberately and systematically, to engage the world and put as much of it under our conscious control as we can manage.

Consider a few examples. Scientists have identified the Higgs boson. Scientists have unraveled the human genome. Engineers have created machines that calculate faster than humans and other machines that diagnose many diseases more reliably than most doctors. Today's scientists track blood flow, electrical current, and many biochemical transitions in the brain. Finally, mathematicians have created fractals, chaos theory, and complexity theory, all of which extend the potency of science to see into reality. Pretty impressive, right?

Scientists and mathematicians aim for the truth about reality, but, as Peirce warned, they can never be sure if and when they have it securely in hand. The Higgs boson does not reveal a unified theory of physics. There is no experimental evidence for any of the proposed string theories. So-called junk DNA between the chromosomes carries much information determining gene expression. "Junk" DNA differentiates us from our nearest primate cousins, chimpanzees and bonobos, by 70 percent (the genetic overlap is somewhere between 92 and 98 percent [Carey, 2015]).

There is more. When it comes to understanding the nature of consciousness and understanding, no speculations are overwhelmingly suggestive. When it comes to artificial intelligence, no one yet knows how to program a computer to think counterfactually or to experience phenomenologically the world as we do (Pearl & MacKenzie, 2018). The mathematics of chaos and complexity seem increasingly to underscore the limits of our ever grasping the truth despite its evident reality (Taleb, 2007). We seem destined to live by approximation.

Peirce's grasp of statistical methods for approximating the ideal of truth proved especially important in his thinking. Peirce believed in both an objective and a subjective interpretation of statistical results (Misak, 2016). Objective probability was ensured by skillful employment of statistical reasoning. Subjective interpretation added to one's rational grounds for relying tentatively on apt summary judgments. Here is Peirce on probability:

> The general problem of probability is, from a given state of facts, to determine the numerical probability of a possible fact. This is the same as to inquire how much the given facts are worth, considered as evidence to prove the possible fact. Thus the problem of probabilities is simply the general problem of logic. (Peirce, 1931–1935, Vol. 3, p. 278)

Peirce knew there were no conclusive grounds to decisively refute the skeptic's persistent challenge, but all representations of reality in the end can be evaluated by their ability to produce extended understanding and control of the world beyond one's own mind. Truth is the ideal that beckons all efforts to know forward. Truth-seeking is as important as ever in Peirce's approach to a theory of knowledge.

In contrast to Peirce's insistence on mathematical rigor wherever possible, fellow pragmatist William James was a bit more relaxed. A physician by trade, James is touted as the founder of American psychology. Like Peirce, James never eschewed truth as an ideal for researchers. However, he did not hold it as an approachable guide to a theory of knowledge, as did Peirce. For Peirce, variance from the ideal of truth was the gauge to the worthiness of conclusions. For James, the worthiness of conclusions showed itself in the satisfaction produced in human judgment and decision-making strategies.

James and Peirce agree that rigorous thinking practices are likely to move people away from avoidable error in the sciences. But James concludes that, in the end, what matters most is the resulting conviction a person has toward a belief or course of action. For James, willing assent, a movement of mind, was the crucial element in a theory of knowledge (James, 1975–1988).

While both believed that pragmatism should be about making the best claims intellectual resources allow in the context of the moment, Peirce. like many others, feared that James's over-emphasis on the psychological may often distract and distort proper knowledge-seeking efforts (Misak, 2008).

James was so committed to the importance of acquired satisfaction as a marker of justified belief that he endorsed decisions to hold religious beliefs, belief in extrasensory perception, and mystical experiences as legitimate sources of knowledge if they led to greater satisfaction in one's encounter with the world. For example, about religion James concludes:

> If religious hypotheses about the universe be in order at all, the active faiths of individuals in them, freely expressing themselves in life, are the experimental tests by which they can be verified, and the only means by which the truth or

falsehood can be wrought out. The truest scientific hypothesis is that which, as we say, "works" best; and it can be no otherwise with religious hypotheses. (James, 1975–1988, vol. 6, p. 8)

Note that despite James favoring satisfaction as the critical element in deciding to adopt a belief, he does not abandon the idea of a truth. Rather, like all pragmatists, James concludes only that guarantees of truth-acquisition are never possible. Even with this caveat in hand, James opines that believing in the truth of an existent God may be so satisfying that given the urgency to decide the issue—one way or another—we are licensed to adopt such conclusions in religion and in the sciences, when the evidence does not decide the issue (Misak, 2018). For James, the urgency of lived experience may require a more rough-and-ready employment of reason. even in the absence of relevant confirming or disconfirming evidence (Misak, 2018).

Just as Peirce and James never backed away from the metaphysical claim that truth exists, neither did the third great pragmatist, John Dewey (Misak, 2013). Like Peirce and James and other disciples of pragmatism, Dewey discouraged both radical skepticism and the quest to grasp truth with certainty. Humans can, and do, learn ways to minimize errors in thinking, evaluation, planning, and so on. The point of a theory of knowledge is to explain how this can best be achieved (Dewey, 1938).

Dewey was not a scientist like Peirce and James. He began as a philosopher much taken with the grandiose pretentions to truth found in the excesses of **Hegelian system-building**. Eventually, Dewey came to recognize it was naïve to expect philosophical systematizing to lead to grand truths. Hegel blended truth and reality into a sort of cosmic mindfulness. This was too much for Dewey to swallow. For Dewey, human agency was ground zero of adept cogitation. Humans had to employ ideas to navigate reality as it was experienced at the moment.

Dewey did not abandon the idea of truth. To do so would require dismissing ideas of right and wrong, good and bad, and many other cognitively distinguishing concepts. Instead, as in the case of the other pragmatists, Dewey set out to develop a theory of knowledge that would most favorably guide human action. For Dewey, as for all pragmatists, context frames the relevant problem space. Successful engagement with the world begins with the here and now as ground zero, not with reflection on some supposed truth-defining principles.

For Dewey, as with the other pragmatists, engagement is a problem-solving challenge. Avoidance of error for Peirce, James, and Dewey is about satisfying established human purpose. For James, avoidance of error also included, at least at times, avoidance of psychological discomfort (James, 1890). This guiding feature of pragmatism—to circumvent error—Dewey found most important in the design, application, and challenging of social and cultural practices, practices inevitable in government and education (Dewey, 1908).

In particular, Dewey contrived a theory of knowledge as a potent energy capable of powering public institutions and organizations generally. Dewey frequently emphasized how experience, when properly attended to, could reveal frameworks for proper guidance (Dewey, 1938). Attention to experience and the challenge at hand can lead the discriminating mind to knowledge satisfactory for fulfilling human purpose at the moment.

Dewey tried to spell out criteria for adjudicating among comparable evaluations of ideas and uses of plans and skills. Beyond the context of theory of knowledge, Dewey's theories about learning, education, and the value of democracy led to extraordinary fame during his own lifetime (Ryan, 1995).

Dewey championed democracy as the only form of state organization sufficiently flexible for parsing truly apt judgments as needed in time and place. Dewey, echoing Aristotle and Plato two millennia earlier, saw education as the key to preparing citizens for participation in a proper state (Siegel, 2017). Plato saw education as preparation for a governing oligarchy. Aristotle recommended education for securing limited democracy. Dewey saw education as key to forming a universal democratic electorate (Dewey, 1907, 1975).

While each of the early pragmatists began with concerns about truth and a default position regarding a theory of knowledge, Dewey increasingly tended to subordinate the theory of knowledge to progressive social planning. Whereas James and, to a lesser extent, Peirce condoned adoption of select beliefs in religion (especially given their soothing effect), Dewey advocated full-scale social engineering to prepare a generation for robust engagement with a world optimizing freedom for all (Dewey, 1975).

Dewey's theory of knowledge extends James's interest in learning strategies in the acquisition of knowledge. Dewey and James brought psychology more prominently into focus within educational thinking. Each believed a theory of knowledge should explain how learning from experience *should* drive apt engagement with the world as it truly is.

PRAGMATISM TODAY, AND ITS COUSINS: SOCIAL CONSTRUCTIONISM AND CONTEXTUALISM

Pragmatism focuses on identifying skills, concepts, and practices that seem to promise the most utility for human decision-making purposes, and these continue to be the focus of pragmatism today (Achinstein, 2019; Elgin, 2017; Scheffler, 1974, 2009). Skills, concepts, and practices are wrong when they systematically frustrate human plans and ambitions. They are saticficing when they accommodate those plans and ambitions. The pragmatist theory of knowledge is about optimizing the fulfillment of human purpose through cautious speculation and rigorous evaluation.

Late-twentieth-century pragmatists Nelson Goodman, Hilary Putnam, and W. V. O. Quine at Harvard each related their work to pragmatism in general and to Dewey especially. Similarly, Richard Rorty at Princeton claimed that theory of knowledge should focus not on insight but on action.

Goodman took up the pragmatic cause when he argued that evaluations of better versus worse can be made not only in the sciences and daily life, but also in the practice and evaluation of the fine and performing arts. The artist's purpose can be fulfilled to a greater or lesser degree in its execution of expression. This, Goodman claims, opens new ways of seeing the world (Goodman, 1978).

Pragmatist Hilary Putnam develops a theory of knowledge often referred to as internal realism. Here the match between the representation and the world need not be isomorphic, but it must allow for purposeful intentions to be realized in the moment of human engagement with the world. When writing, often along with his wife, philosopher Ruth Putnam, Putnam makes explicit that he sees their work as derivative from Dewey (Putnam & Putnam, 1993).

Finally, W. V. O. Quine, addressing scientific knowledge in particular, argues that theories about the world can be made optimally suggestive, but go no further (Quine, 1953). Quine identifies Dewey as an originator of this sort of approach to knowledge. However, like Peirce, Quine never denies that there can be a perfect match between reality and a representation of reality. Rather, like Peirce, he asserts we will never know if such **isomorphisms** exist (Quine, 1953).

Another pragmatic theory of knowledge, is *instrumentalism*. Here scientific theories are best thought of not as pictures of reality, but rather as tools—instruments—for organizing experience and helping make successful predictions. In instrumentalism, as in pragmatism generally, the idea of capturing truth is set aside as an ideal. Instrumentalists in particular emphasize how the tools of logic and science can manage apt engagement with the world more effectively than less disciplined thinking.

Finally, an extreme variant of pragmatism is descended from the work of Richard Rorty. Rorty claims that focusing on action addresses all human needs as best anyone can hope. Rorty sums up his position: "It is action that sets destiny and not expert thinking about the truly 'real'" (Rorty, 1990, p. 2). This summing has led to *social constructionism*.

In contrast to Thomas Kuhn, as mentioned in chapter 1, Rorty embraces a robust social constructionism. Rorty sees social constructionism as an unavoidable default position in the absence of successful attempts to guarantee the capture of truth (Rorty, 2015). Since truth cannot be captured, Rorty argues that human satisfaction with ways of seeing suffice as the goal of knowledge. This unbridled adoption of human satisfaction as the sole criterion for acceptable knowledge claims takes the theory of knowledge far beyond the satisficing efforts of the more modest pragmatists mentioned (Rorty, 1982).

Like Rorty, social constructionists in general tend to find the concept of truth bothersome. To these social constructionists, if truth is inaccessible, then there is no reason to consider it relevant to a theory of knowledge. Thinking about the world need not, and in fact cannot, extend further than identifying beliefs that groups are willing to abide. Knowledge is a social construct and nothing more. There is no getting closer to something deservedly called truth. For social constructionists, a theory of knowledge is limited to the implicit and explicit beliefs and commitments that bind people in communal engagements with one another. New beliefs are acquired as a result of emerging psychological inclinations on the part of some in interaction with others. Privileged beliefs result from social dynamics rather than from accurate observation and astute reasoning. Consequently, there is no purpose in seeking anything other than social cohesion (Berger & Luckmann, 1966).

Seeking little more than social cohesion can lead to some very unfortunate encounters with both the material world and even with other non-agreeing humans. A population acting in group-think fashion can err in seriously self-destructive ways when there is no check beyond consensus on the wisdom of such action. Social constructionists cannot escape the fact that with no ideal beyond satisfying transient human purpose, they are at risk of escalating error of all sorts. In contrast, more mainstream pragmatists aim at minimizing avoidable error.

TRUTH EXISTS, BUT DOES IT REALLY MATTER?

When Catherine Elgin writes that rationality unavoidably aims for knowledge, she aligns with pragmatists who take seriously the idea that one can know that an apt search for plausibility diminishes the likelihood of avoidable error in thinking, judgment, and planning (Elgin, 2017). Elgin sympathizes with mainstream pragmatism or what one might call *pragmatic realism*. Pragmatic realism is reflected in Thomas Kuhn's declaration to Wagner described in chapter 1: "I am a physicist for gosh sakes. Of course I think there is a world out there. And, I think we can be right or wrong about that world."

Elgin warns social constructionists generally and relativists in particular about a priori dogmatism in a theory of knowledge: "Dogmatism requires closing our minds to new evidence, lest knowledge will be lost. Rationality [the search for the ideal of truth] requires keeping an open mind" (Elgin, 2017, p. 297). Minds are closed when at the outset of any investigation, the existence of truth and approachability of truth is denied.

The resources of human rationality are bounded, as Nobel Laureate Herbert Simon concluded long ago. That boundedness encompasses both neurological and cultural constraints. Still, as philosopher Tyler Burge aptly points out, if humans were not able to muster their collective wisdom in an increasingly successful fashion to avoid relentless error, the species would have ceased to exist long ago (Burge, 2010). But, pragmatically speaking, the boundedness of rationality limits the range of cognitive resources but not the possibility of limiting avoidable error.

There is surely a class of beliefs that stand above the beliefs of mere tradition, eccentric imaginings, and group-think. People do things that, upon reflection, appear to them to be stupid or even irrational. Groups of people find their way to embarrassing errors of all sorts. Equally evident is the track record of humans avoiding ever-greater ranges of error as they pursue ever more refined and systematic investigations into the workings of the world.

SUMMARY, RECOMMENDATIONS, AND CAVEATS

Summary

Pragmatism is a robust approach to theory of knowledge. But to be *pragmatically useful*, professionals embracing the concept of pragmatism must understand it more deeply than many do today. To understand pragmatism more deeply, here are a few important takeaways.

1. Pragmatism does not deny the existence of truth.
2. Pragmatism discourages dogmatic assertions that may mislead people into thinking they have captured absolute truths.
3. Pragmatism is committed to the avoidance of unnecessary error in human thinking, planning, and action.
4. Pragmatism shuns metaphysical and absolutist claims about the nature of truth.
5. Because of its respect for the existence of truth, pragmatism should never be seen as closely aligned with radical skepticism, nihilism, or extreme social constructionism.
6. The strategy and goal of pragmatism is to guide thinkers away from unnecessary risk when drawing conclusions and making plans.

Recommendations

1. Pragmatic thinking encompasses any and all systematic approaches to problem-solving that show promise. Thus, pragmatists should learn commonsense strategies for social engagement with others, decision and game theory for managing both personal and institutional operations, and become familiar with various scientific strategies for truth-seeking.
2. Pragmatists must focus attention on context and problem space prior to seeking solutions or evaluating recommendations.
3. Pragmatists should never act on mere opinion. Reflective deliberation is an important must for all "slow thinking" decision-making projects.
4. Pragmatists track plans implemented and all relevant decisions and judgments to ensure plans and actions are working, and not just hope that the immediate future will distract from looming unsolved challenges.

Caveats

1. Think twice about the reasons for a challenge vanishing. Pragmatists want to know their solutions are effective. A challenge may disappear for any number of reasons having nothing to do with an administrator's or a scientist's good thinking. Pragmatists double-check their work to track effectiveness in their planning, both before and after the fact.
2. Unintended consequences are always a threat in context-shifting situations. Pragmatists give special consideration to the possibility of unintended consequences.
3. Pragmatists must recognize that purpose and context must be clearly aligned in order to effectively address a problem space.

Chapter Four

Policy-Makers and Administrators as Contextualists and Pragmatists

FEEDING THE STAKEHOLDERS PROPORTIONATELY

You saw in chapter 3 that the pragmatist cause began with a search for truth. While pragmatists came to agree that there could be no capture and no guarantee that truth could be captured, the pragmatists never dismissed truth as a phantom of some sort. For example, Peirce continued to focus attention on truth by insisting that knowledge evolves, approaching ever closer to truth, even though we would never recognize truth even if we found it (Ayer, 1968).

In addition, James and Dewey found license for knowing assertions in cases such as religious belief, where supporting evidence was out of reach, but the urgency to conclude something regarding the supernatural may lead to conviction based on the strength of will or the need to decide what to believe (Misak, 2016; Kvanvig, 2018). Even Peirce seemed ready to accept provisional license in matters of religion (Aikin, 2014).

The refusal to disavow the existence of truth continued among most pragmatists throughout the twentieth century, and it continues in the work of thinkers such as Achinstein (2019) and Elgin (2017). As pragmatism has become more demanding of rigorous strategies for avoiding error in judgment, planning, and thinking, it has become increasingly appealing to scholars from the sciences and the humanities (Kraut, 1990).

Pragmatism has also acquired a fan base of nonspecialists who self-describe as pragmatists but who seem to understand little, if anything, of it as a theory of knowledge. These self-described pragmatists are often reckless, shoot-from-the-hip mavericks who simply claim a personal excellence in problem-solving. At best their claims are merited—if at all—by a community shift in its attention to a previously assessed problem. As noted in the previous chapter, a problem vanishing is not evidence of skillful solution.

There are many examples in education of programs, large and small, that were implemented under the guise of securing accountability, thereby supposedly ensuring a solution to some ill-defined problem. An ill-defined problem in education often shows up as little more than a lament. For example, bemoaning that "students are not learning all they should" neither defines nor explains what should be learned or why. Later in this chapter, the standardized testing cure for the nation's education problems is discussed at some length as an example of a *nonpragmatic* action initiative.

Claiming pragmatic credibility when addressing real-world problems does not in itself make a policy pragmatic, nor a policy-maker a pragmatist. Since pragmatism is first and foremost a theory of knowledge, the intellectual challenge must be addressed in substantive detail. Expert laments and public opinion polls do not outline intellectual challenges in substantive detail.

For example, there is a concern about an alleged "global achievement gap" (T. Wagner, 2008). Genuine pragmatists define what students should learn and further explain why, in a given context, this is the material that should be learned. Genuine pragmatists would describe the intellectual challenge by identifying the relevant context and the social engineering required to change that context for the better.

The social engineering required will follow the contours of the challenge and will involve accountability measures and feedback loops driving action towards expectations. However, despite all these conscientious measures, pragmatists must acknowledge, as psychologist D. T. Campbell warns, the likelihood of unintended negative consequences and the shifting sands of social realities (Campbell, 1975).

This may sound straightforward. But, too often, the follow-through is flawed. Often the flaw is in the original envisioning of a concern. In the absence of focus and with the failure to respect the idea that there could be approachable truths, policies and protocols cannot be reasonably designed for skillful improvements in any given social context.

Below is a sketch of No Child Left Behind (NCLB) and Every Student Succeeds Act (ESSA) policies to "fix" education. This sketch is utilized to show how, in the absence of pragmatic criteria, such initiatives lead to increased risk of error. Genuine pragmatists are systematic and comprehensive in their evaluation in ways that elude shoot-from-the-hip problem-solvers despite their claim to the mantle of pragmatism.

BEWARE OF THE SWAGGERIST

Everyone has come across a politician, a policy-maker, an administrator, or a boss who prides himself on being an instant problem-solver. These folks often describe themselves as pragmatists, yet it is rarely the case that these self-anointed experts and leaders give much thought to concepts of truth and theory of knowledge. Their ambitions are not to figure out solutions, but rather to figure out how to make a problem go away. Those two ambitions are not identical. Caveat: if it swaggers, it is not analyzing, evaluating, and deciding responsibly.

The swaggerist profile described above has not gone unnoticed by other authors who have on occasion described such profiles as "ham-fisted pragmatists" (Kvanvig, 2018). In organizations of all sorts individuals with sufficient power often run amok, and in so doing they fracture shared purpose and diminish successful cooperation, all the while applauding their own "pragmatism."

How swaggerists come to power could be an interesting empirical study. Most likely such studies will involve the triangulating of several models. However, inasmuch as the purpose here is merely to distinguish the swaggerist claiming to be a pragmatist from a person who genuinely is pragmatic, there will no attempt to venture into those details.

Swaggerists tend to disparage truth-seeking early on. Swaggerists often declare that "everyone has their own truth." The advantage to swaggerists in making such claims is it gives them license to act with a degree of abandon because they do not see criteria for truth as impediments to their decisions. When all is relative to the fits and fancies of the group, the person with the greatest control gets to announce "the truth." Might makes right in this view—but this is not genuine pragmatism.

Swaggerists tend to view the world as made of problems to be solved, coupled with win/lose taxonomies. When problems vanish for whatever reason, the swaggerist considers them no longer a problem. True enough. But misleadingly, the swaggerist often considers the vanquished problem solved. Mere dissolution of problems is not pragmatic success.

Swaggerist disparagement of truth leads as well to the disparagement of truth-seeking strategies. Swaggerists tend to license their own hunches as credible solutions in a truth-free environment wherein abrupt action and "might makes right" policy-making serve as sufficient guides for all relevant progress. In contrast, pragmatists are wary of self-initiated error and seek counsel often, recognizing the acquired expertise of some experts over others.

Swaggerists use committees and outside advisers only to the extent that they reinforce the swaggerists' hunches or can be targeted for blame in the absence of success. In contrast, pragmatists seek appropriate advisors to diminish the risk of self-imposed, prejudicial error.

In viewing the world as a set of problems and win or lose as the outcome, swaggerists turn their backs on fundamental pragmatist commitments. First and foremost, swaggerists are oblivious to the idea that pragmatism is a theory of knowledge. As such, pragmatism begins, not with problems narrowly defined, but rather with intellectual challenges broadly defined. Addressing intellectual challenges may require strategies in which components are broken into more manageable problem sets but this is a pragmatic strategy, not a definition of pragmatism.

The breadth of pragmatism means that pragmatists address intellectual challenges that require intelligence, but do not have a win/lose outcome to be secured. This breadth allows pragmatism to serve educators and others across a broad expanse of intellectual challenges and not just immediate problems begging for solutions. Consider the following example.

A successful principal at a parochial school may have a lucrative offer of a principalship at a troubled inner-city public school. Should she take the job?

She readily acknowledges that holding either job represents an achievement in life to be proud of and find satisfying, each in its own way. There is no right or wrong answer here. In fact, there is no better answer or worse answer. And given the way things are in her life at the moment, there is no need that the one job better fulfills than the other. Yet she faces a choice. She will not flip a coin and leave things to the fates. She wants to think this through as best she can—a very pragmatic start.

There is so much to consider. She loves the faculty, students, and atmosphere at her current school. The school has limited resources and limited financial incentives for personnel. The school is small, but it has an intimate community feeling that pervades every classroom and every activity.

On the other hand, she likes a challenge. And, while she does not need the money, a substantial increase in pay is always attractive. She knows she may not succeed in the large, urban environment. The public school is unionized, and she knows no one there. Yet that is all part of what defines the adventure. She likes equally the urban adventure on the one hand, and on the other, the intimacy of her current school community. What she faces is not a problem, properly speaking, but rather an intellectual challenge to be decided rightly.

There is no set of preferences and likely outcomes in this case that make one decision more likely to be right. Making a list, weighting and comparing evaluations like Ben Franklin once advised a young suitor asking for his advice about whether to marry, will not do (Wagner et al., 2018). A weighted list in such circumstances may be a good start, but it is only a start. Moreover, the process of *properly* giving weight to the varied considerations is enormously challenging—a fact pragmatists appreciate, but swaggerists do not.

The principal's dilemma is not a merely matter of placing the best bet in the circumstances. There is no more probably right decision to be made. So, how can she best know what to do? The early pragmatists point out that some decisions must be made in the absence of abundant evidential indicators (Kvanvig, 2018). Usually they had in mind matters of religious commitment, but the lack of sure evidence for the best decision seems equally the case here.

All problems are intellectual challenges, but not all intellectual challenges are problems. Here the principal faces an intellectual challenge. Whereas a swaggerist might abruptly say, "Show me the money!" and go with that decision or "Stay where you are safe. Don't take chances," the pragmatist appreciates that understanding in such situations requires more diligent attention.

The pragmatist will encourage the principal to look further for counsel. What do family and friends think, given what they know about her. What are the possible consequences of things going wrong in either choice? What is the likelihood of those negative consequences?

Problems that disappear are testimony to the swaggerist's handling of things. In this case, if the job offer is suddenly withdrawn or the parochial school goes bankrupt, the problem is solved! Certainly pragmatists will agree the challenge at hand no longer exists, but they would not rack up the outcome as a systematically and responsibly derived solution.

To pragmatists, challenges come and go, but approximate solutions are evident only when context-responsive solutions are systematically evaluated. To systematically evaluate a solution requires alert attention to the details of the pragmatic theory of knowledge. These details include: sufficiently exhaustive description of context, apt identification of available resources, likelihood of strategic success, costs of right or wrong decisions in the impending context, and clear identification of acceptable grounds for declaring intended success.

The differences between swaggerists and authentic pragmatists are most vivid in moral and social challenges. Imagine a teacher is accused of some heinous act. Imagine too that the teacher is unpopular with other teachers and staff. Imagine the local press shooting from the hip and demanding the teacher's immediate dismissal. Think about it. What makes the problem go away the fastest? What is a swaggerist likely to do? What would you expect an authentic pragmatist to do?

Responsible politicians, policy-makers, administrators, and other authorities must give some thought to how we can truly know things—the theory of knowledge—before drawing conclusions or executing a practice in order to be true to their professed pragmatism. Hunches, opinions, rumors, biases, prejudices, and other expediencies are tools of swaggerists but not of authentic pragmatists. Acquiring genuine knowledge, making discriminating evaluations, and calculating a range of risks are all things that a theory of knowledge envelops, and those things place demands on pragmatists that they are never at license to ignore.

Anyone in authority, including teachers, can be either a swaggerist or a pragmatist. But, as a class, the stakeholders focused on in this chapter tend to be people who embrace something they readily call pragmatism. To simplify the taxonomy among this class of stakeholders in education, this chapter will proceed by generalizing about some effective as well as ineffective uses of pragmatic principles.

However, the reader should be aware that there is no intention to divide all members of this stakeholder class into some bifurcated taxonomy. Rather, think of the distinction between swaggerists and authentic pragmatists as being on a spectrum. Hopefully, most stakeholders at this level are not so extreme as to deserve the label "swaggerist." Similarly, there are presumably few so intellectual and talented to be deserving of the accolade fully authentic pragmatist.

For various reasons involving personal skill, institutional culture, level of training, and so on, stakeholders at this level embrace the general nomenclature of pragmatism despite wide variation in their commitment to the principles of this theory of knowledge.

CAMPBELL'S LAW AND NCLB, ESSA, AND THEIR COUSINS

A large-scale example of pragmatically driven concerns for these stakeholders is exemplified in the development and management of state and local programs affiliated with NCLB and then ESSA on the national level. A public concern about the state of the nation's education system led policymakers at the very highest level of American democracy to grasp anything that seemed able to ease the public's lament (Merrow, 2017; Cohen et al., 2017).

Initially, the federal government commissioned a study to determine what shape the nation's schools were truly in. That report, titled *A Nation at Risk*, began by stating, "If another government had done to our schools what we ourselves have done we would declare it an act of war" (National Commission on Excellence in Education, 1983).

Individual states began testing programs that they thought would monitor and then lead to the improvement of public education (Linn et al., 2002). What happened in Texas and, more specifically, Houston is especially revealing (Hoffman et al., 2001). Dr. Rod Paige was the Houston Independent School District's superintendent at the time. Paige was quick to catch on to the demand for accountability. He was absorbed in management jargon.

He put the district on a demanding program of standardized testing and threatened dismissal of teachers whose classes failed to improve. The goal for HISD was a 10 percent improvement in scores every year. One does not need a degree in mathematics or research methodology to realize that this was an aim reaching beyond 100 percent improvement with no end in sight. Was that laudable, or just naïve?

George W. Bush was the Texas governor at the time. He became infatuated with Paige's results-driven program for improving education. Bush made Paige's program the Texas state standard and then, when Bush became president, he made Paige his Secretary of Education. A short time later the nation was dealing with a program endorsed by Democrats as fully as by Republicans. Teachers were going to get their students test scores up, or else! Increases in test score means increases in education (McDonnell & Weatherford, 2016).

Promoters of No Child Left Behind thought of it as a "no-nonsense approach" to repairing the problems of education. These were "pragmatic" leaders claiming to fix the problem now. They eschewed lofty ivory tower theories. First, they found a problem: education. Then they showed a quantitative improvement on some sort of standardized test, and then they could declare the problem solved (Berliner, 2006; Berliner & Biddle, 1995; Berliner & Glass, 2014; Darling-Hammond, 2013; Ravitch, 2020). So, where did this inept and inauthentic pragmatism lead the nation's education?

W. Edwards Deming, a physicist and senior architect of Total Quality Management (TQM), helped to turn Japan into an international economic powerhouse. Known for his focus on the accuracy of quality control measurement, Deming had a theory of knowledge that was robustly pragmatic in the authentic sense (Deming, 2000, 2018).

Throughout the NCLB years, a few attempts at TQM were tried (Wong et al., 2009). But even Deming's own recommendations fell flat. The reasons NCLB could not replicate the robust success of TQM in Japanese industry are numerous. At the head of the list is a failure of NCLB to embody a consensual theory of knowledge for defining educational success. TQM was based on clear-cut quantitative units that could be measured and tracked. NCLB policy-makers assumed education and schooling practices could be measured and evaluated in the same way.

NCLB grasped at students' standardized test scores as the units defining measurement of schooling success. But education is about so much more than students' ability to recognize the likely right answer out of four alternatives on a multiple-choice test. The advantage of standardized tests is that they can be graded, summed, and compared in discrete fashion. An increase in test scores, given the impoverished assumptions of NCLB about knowledge, meant that education was getting better. The "problem of education" was presumably being fixed.

There are so many problems with this alleged fix that researchers have identified over the years, such that scores of articles and dozens of scholarly books have been written. The issues raised include gender disparity, racial disparities, test biases, and numerous technical aspects identified by statisticians and research methodologists (Oakes, 2017; Rothstein et al., 2008; Strauss, 2016). But few highlight the failure to understand a pragmatist theory of knowledge and consequences of such failures.

For example, Deming warned policy-makers to be wary of overconfidence in the numbers they collect and evaluate. People are very good at delivering the numbers required, so the numbers required better be the most relevant to institutional success (Deming, 2018).

An added caveat from Deming was to drive out fear (Deming, 2000, 2018). If people fear personal consequences for meeting measurement targets, then sure enough, they will find a way to manufacture the data, even at the cost of the organization's health. This is exactly what happened with No Child Left Behind. NCLB wanted all children to improve beyond a minimal level as measured on a standardized test. This meant curricula around the country immediately shrank in order to become test focused. It no longer mattered how much students *genuinely* learned. Rather, what mattered in the end was the percentage of students hurdling the mandated standard. This had a tendency both to compromise the educational opportunities of the very bright and to demean the efforts of dedicated teachers working with extremely low-performing students.

Taking students who easily meet the basic standard and teaching them as much as one can was not rewarded by the new NCLB, or the subsequent ESSA focus (Jennings & Rentner, 2006; Koretz, 2005; Ladd, 2017; Ladson-Billings, 2006; Lee & Reeves, 2012). In addition, students who were far below the basic standard but more than doubled their scores at the hands of an earnest, hard-working teacher still counted as failures—that is, their achievement was a failure for the students themselves, for their teachers, and for their schools. Is that fair? Does that make sense?

Should part of education involve role-modeling sincerity and fairness to students? Should integrity in measuring actual teacher success with individual students matter? How are these things being measured?

Predictably, cheating on tests has become a widespread problem (Takahashi, 2014; Toppo et al., 2011; Upton et al., 2011; Vogell, 2011). And it is not a problem of the occasional soft-hearted teacher monitoring a test and giving a hard-working student a helpful nudge now and again. The cheating has been large-scale by teachers, administrators, and policy-makers.

In Rod Paige's Houston Independent School District there was a cheating scandal in the Sharpstown area schools where administrators encouraged test manipulation on the part of subordinates. And here, nearly 20 years post-Paige, the Houston School District is in danger of being taken over by the state of Texas (Amrein-Beardsley & Collins, 2012) because of too many schools performing poorly on tests. In other attempts to "beat the system,"

Latino students dropping out were told to fill out the papers saying they were leaving the country so that their dropouts would not be counted against school and district totals.

The problems with Houston's school district are similar to many major school districts (Booher-Jennings, 2005; Gartner, 2012), but they are small potatoes compared to some of the most egregious efforts of administrators to deliver the right numbers. In El Paso, the superintendent of schools, who had been named the nation's superintendent of the year, was arrested and is now in prison for large-scale manipulation of test scores (Fernandez, 2012). And he is not alone among senior administrators risking all to achieve numeric expectations.

In Washington DC, Michelle Rhee, the school system chancellor who had gained national praise for her ham-fisted "pragmatic" firing of teachers, resigned after floundering in the midst of wide-scale cheating among district teachers (Brown, 2013; Gillum & Bello, 2011). Meanwhile, one teacher she fired became teacher of the year in a wealthy nearby school district a year later (Koretz, 2015)! Similarly, in Atlanta, where another ham-fisted "pragmatist" was praised for getting tough with teachers, that superintendent was also found to be awash in irregularities of data reporting (Blinder, 2015; Judd, 2012a; 2012b).

The fact of the matter is that episodes of cheating seem ubiquitous based on the reporting in national news outlets (Holland, 2012; Jacob & Levitt, 2003). In addition, comparing American student performance on the Programme for International Student Assessment (PISA) tests with international students shows that standardized testing required by NCLB and continued under ESSA has led to no comparative gains versus other nations, except possibly in a couple of elementary school subjects (Koretz, 2015). With or without cheating, the "problem of education" is not being fixed by the so-called pragmatists' own standards (Jones, 2007).

In addition to all these episodes of cheating, experts such as Daniel Koretz, Diane Ravitch, David Berliner, and Linda Darling-Hammond raise questions about the practice of teacher coaching, in which students are taught schemes for increasing the odds of picking an answer in the midst of ignorance (Berliner, 2006; Darling-Hammond, 2013; Koretz, 2015; Ravitch, 2010). This coaching demeans the nobility of becoming educated by reducing education for both teachers and students to nothing more than a numbers game. As Deming warned: people are uncannily good at delivering the numbers they are asked to deliver.

In his book, *The Testing Charade*, Daniel Koretz documents cases of administrators who were praised by stakeholders for securing consensus toward plans of circumventing or even falsifying student scores on standardized examinations. At the local level, all were happy for a while that test scores were no longer such a burden. However, when the scam began to unravel, what seemed like a good idea became severely disruptive to the social climate of schools and districts. Heads would roll (Koretz, 2017, pp. 111–118).

These practices demonstrate, sadly, the continuing relevance of D. T. Campbell's law: "The more any quantitative social indicator is used for social decision-making, the more subject it will be to corruption pressures and the more apt it will be to distort and corrupt the social processes it is intended to monitor" (Campbell, 1975).

GENUINE CONCERN ABOUT EDUCATION

This analysis only scratches the surface of all that is wrong with NCLB and ESSA. Ideas like developing autonomy, critical thinking, independent evaluation of truth claims, social practices leading to in-depth knowledge, and the nobility of becoming educated were all ignored by the high-handed theorists and bosses who rushed to rescue the country from a problem whose context was never well defined in the first place.

The most serious problem is that no one took the time to bring everyone on board to a reasonable definition of education or to criteria of truth for what we hope to approach through education. There was no agreement among stakeholders about what they thought they knew about the nature, function, and purpose of education. Philip Jackson wrote a little book during this period on what education is. He initially wrote as Deweyan disciple, and he laid a rationale for seeing education in a certain light (Jackson, 2012).

Jackson's rationale largely fell on deaf ears. As noted above, stakeholders at Level 1 have one notion of truth in education. It can be accommodated by genuine theorists at Level 2, but, unfortunately, Level 2 has fallen into the hands not of theorists, but rather those who brashly rush to solve a problem—even one not well defined. With no well-defined problem and no well-defined context, there is no point to any talk of approaching a solution to the so-called problem.

The missing definitions of the problem and the context alluded to above must be in alignment at least in some fashion with what and how stakeholders appraise the truth of the situation. Definitions cannot do much for something that is little more than a vague public lament crossing multiple levels of stakeholders.

Evaluating truth claims requires some theory about what knowledge truly is. Evaluating truth claims requires some skills and dispositions for pursuing a line of inquiry aimed at establishing a degree of plausibility. Not a single standardized test aims at detecting the development of these skills and dispositions in students.

Even if there is some disparity among stakeholder groups about the most fitting theory of knowledge, when everyone's cards are on the table, there is hope for consensual progress. But if relevant theories of knowledge are ignored by major stakeholder groups and if mention of truth is avoided, there is little for stakeholders on which to share assent (Wagner & Simpson, 2008).

Oddly, since standardized tests focus so heavily on recognition responses, they appear to be better suited for use in a long-ago past. Think about it—most fourth graders now have access to smartphones and computers that give them instant access to an amount of stored information greater than that of a dozen 70-year-old scholars. Why should education be viewed as a matter of memory recall?

Scholars and scientists who serve as the champions of successful education around the world have always been those who stood apart from the crowd. These champions proved themselves by asking questions few had considered before. They proved their mettle by sticking with a line of inquiry until it made sense even in the face of withering criticism by previous masters. Yet none of this is the focus of most state programs to improve education today.

Recall that authentic pragmatists do not go about viewing the world as simply a set of problems to be solved. Authentic pragmatists are ever-alert to intellectual challenges of understanding. Intellectual challenges are more than a mere content-driven lament. Policy-makers concluded there was a public lament about the state of education. They rushed to solve the problem before they studied the context.

There may well have been a broad-based lament regarding public education, but that did not mean there was a single thing that all wanted fixed. One good thing about the last 30 years of reform is that it has uncovered dissent regarding public education coming from many sectors. Instead of a single lament that needed a singular address, it now appears that there are many expectations of stakeholders and many separate aspects of educational practice that merit comprehensive address (Cuban, 2013).

To the hard-charging "pragmatist" if the public lament is eased, the problem should be viewed as being solved. Yet as was seen in Washington D. C. and elsewhere, dramatic action and subsequent data reporting can be misleading for a number of reasons (Dee & Jacob, 2011; DeWolf & Janssens, 2007). In contrast, for genuine pragmatists, what has been accumulating is a host of problems that need to be addressed, and there is no "one size fits all" solution to the current set of problems in public education.

Certainly, one crisis that most educational pragmatists would rally around is the need for students to learn more and better skills and dispositions for tackling intellectual challenges in both daily and academic life (Giroux, 2013; Koretz, 2017). But even here, a good context-driven pragmatist knows that truth-seeking in biology is not the same as truth-seeking in say, mathematics. The dispositions and skills of figuring things out vary, sometimes widely, among the various disciplines.

Improvement at figuring things out and advancing personal autonomy is more central to a genuine pragmatic theory of knowledge and its role in education than either making students better at recognition items or, more generally, making some perceived problem disappear.

Smartphones can stand in for much that needs to be memorized, but smartphones cannot stand in for evaluation and critical review of plans, theories, actions, protocols, and policies. Test-aligned standardized rubrics might be better for measuring the sufficiency of smartphones than for measuring students' skills and dispositions for figuring things out or for measuring their growing capacities for the exercise of personal autonomy.

NCLB and ESSA do not provide the only examples of self-proclaimed pragmatists going the way of overconfident bosses. It is simply the most conspicuous example evident on the grandest of scales (Caplan, 2018; Koretz, 2005).

The problem of state and local boards of education and administrators—from superintendents to department chairs—claiming license for their decisions as "good old-fashioned pragmatism" is widespread, as is evident in the case of Michelle Rhee and others (Thurston et al., 2015; Toppo, 2013).

There is good reason for stakeholders at Level 2 to embrace pragmatism as a theory of knowledge, but simply claiming to be pragmatic is not a license to "shoot from the hip" in virtue of one's position of power (Carnoy & Loeb, 2003; Culpepper, 2017; Grant, 2012).

AN INTENSE SEARCH FOR AN IDEAL

So, what makes authentic pragmatism such an apt theory of knowledge for stakeholders at this level of educational practice?

The largest group of stakeholders are found in Level 1. These stakeholders expect stakeholders in Level 2 to exhibit competency and understanding, leading the way toward ever-greater success in all types of training and education. Level 2 stakeholders are surely of one mind in wanting to satisfy the expectations of Level 1 stakeholders. So, where is there a problem?

First, the ordering of the pragmatic challenge should not be as listed above: competency and understanding. Rather it is *understanding* that turns abilities into demonstrable capabilities. There is a rich evolving literature on the transition of abilities into capabilities (Bailin & Battersby, 2017; Bradford, 2015), but we can circumvent that for now by simply emphasizing that one must understand what one is up to before one can competently engage in needed action.

Furthermore, understanding is far from a reflex and far from Nobel Laureate Daniel Kahneman's description of "fast thinking" protocols. Intellectual challenges from mundane problem-solving to theory construction and policy-making requires what Kahneman describes as "slow thinking." Slow thinking is a matter of figuring things out as opposed to racing toward a decision (Kahneman, 2011).

Authentic pragmatists surely have no problem with fast-thinking in context, but when problem-solving, theory-making, and policy construction is at issue, slow thinking is unavoidable and the responsible thing to do. Expediency and reaction time is not what any Law of Figuring Things Out requires. The Law of Figuring Things Out requires attention to *all* the resources of decision sciences and critical evaluation (Wagner et al., 2018).

If there were no such thing as truth, there would be no sense in speaking of understanding. Even if the human mind or each individual human mind were isolated from all else in the world, confined solely in its own imaginings, identifying that phenomenon would be a truth. There is no escape from truth for a thoroughgoing pragmatist. Recall that not one of the pragmatists described in the previous chapter spoke in terms of capturing truth. Instead, their theory of knowledge, when properly understood, approaches truth solely by means of moving away from error.

Truth for the pragmatist is typically an unattainable ideal. Reaching for truth, in contrast, is both attainable and well worth the effort. In the process of truth-seeking the pragmatist identifies and removes degrees and patches of error from her thinking when all goes well. When the pragmatist Catherine Elgin titles her recent book *True Enough*, she is not endorsing shoot-from-the-hip decision-making but rather increasing expertise in error identification and error avoidance in the process of truth-seeking (Elgin, 2017).

Authentic pragmatism is well-suited to stakeholder ambitions at this level. But, keep in mind, true pragmatists never confuse mere personal ambition with the ideal of truth-seeking utilizing skill, dispositions, and background knowledge relevant to the challenge (Coburn et al., 2016; Coles, 2003).

True pragmatists embrace a theory of knowledge that requires defining and redefining relevant context. True pragmatism embraces what we have previously called the Law of Figuring Things Out (Wagner et al., 2018). This law requires that the full extent of resources in critical thinking and the decision sciences be employed to address an increasingly well-defined challenge. True pragmatists are confident that, when they abide by these directives, the likelihood of moving away from error increases. In short, there is an approach to approximate truth that is realizable.

MAKING THINGS HAPPEN

If the pragmatist theory of knowledge leads to such promising results, why does education stumble along as it does?

One obvious reason has already been mentioned. Not all who declare themselves and their actions as licensed by pragmatism are thinking or acting like genuine pragmatists. These swaggerists are usually acting in the absence of any theory of knowledge at all. They fly by the seat of their pants and gamble on what seems most plausible to them at the moment.

Then too, there are so-called social constructionists. They are not true pragmatists, despite being mistaken for such on the faulty assumption that pragmatists and social constructionists share a relativist approach to truth. Of course, as noted at length previously, pragmatists are neither relativists nor social constructionists by any stretch of the imagination. Pragmatists acknowledge the reality of truth as much as they acknowledge that it is generally inaccessible to appropriation.

Pragmatists have a theory of knowledge, and it begins with identifying the context of an intellectual challenge. Subsequently, context and human purpose and ambition are considered together. Then, context is again considered and usually broadened in order to give a more comprehensive view of the actual challenge being undertaken.

Above we noted that a lament about the current state of education is no statement of problem or challenge. Too many interest groups and the three levels of stakeholders all have focus points that agitate them about this or that educational practice. Consequently, in the absence of operable definitions of the challenge, both large-scale reformative efforts and many small ones flounder.

Time and again, whether blame is aimed at current policy, inept administration, incompetent teachers, or uninvolved parents, the solution seems very nearly always the same: more accountability. Produce numbers to force the offending factors out. Then, time and again, this does not work because simply making tougher and more accurate measurements will not solve complications inherent in any large-scale social engineering practice.

This seemingly inexhaustible push to always do more of the same has led to extreme measures to ensure test and curriculum "alignment," that is, teaching to the test. It leads to a rubric specificity that breaks all instruction into the tiniest fragments imaginable; then the results are taught to students in a bit-by-bit fashion. Again, this never works, but is always the base for reform at the hands of so-called pragmatists.

Imagine, for just a moment, that you are about to learn to play the board game Monopoly. Children around the world learn to play the game in a matter of minutes. Usually it works like this. A few children know how to play. They tell you how to play, explain the pieces, and add a couple of tips about strategy. Then with no further ado you start play and learn more along the way. Is there accountability in this approach?

The accountability is evident in now knowing how to play. But imagine how the game would be taught using standard teaching practices based on standardized testing as a measure of success. Have you ever read the instructions on the inside of the Monopoly board box? Pretty daunting right?

So standard teaching would break those instructions into a set of lesson plans, each exhibiting incredibly detailed rubrics for timely multiple-choice testing after each lesson. Then, keeping lessons to a standardized 40 minutes a day to allow for an end-of-the-day quiz. It would take at least a week to take students through the instructions and pass a final exam on playing Monopoly. The numbers do not lie. We would know . . . well, exactly what would we know?

We would know what percentage of students passed the final. But just because the final is aligned with the instructions and game, does that also mean that students would know how to play the game if they got a passing score? What about two weeks later, would they still know how to play the game? If students were taught Monopoly in this fashion, how many do you think would ever want to play this long-standing favorite board game ever again! Why can the all-too-oblivious "pragmatists" not learn from such examples?

The world of learning is full of examples just like this, but too few reformers learn from them (Duncan, 2010). Everyone who went to public school came across a percentage of "poor students" who got bad grades and often dropped out. They were looked down on as failures. Yet a significant number of those so-called failures live very well by fixing the Mercedes, the air conditioners, and other electrical and plumbing gadgetry that their former classmates who became doctors and lawyers cannot fix themselves. Read your new car manual! Fixing a car is not easy.

And yet there is more. A number of these poor students participated in some kind of vocational training. During that training they may have been submitted to the same test–and–measure protocol. They may learn how to replace a condenser, but they may not be very good at understanding why that is the problem your car or home air conditioner is experiencing. In contrast, in rural America it is amazing at times to find people with little education who can fix any car or tractor, household appliance, or farm implement, while they raise crops and tend to ailing animals. How did they learn so much?

Genuine pragmatists have been trying to tell the world how that happens for over 100 years now! These people aim at getting things right. They believe in the truth of the matter, even if it cannot be known for certain. They experiment with real possibilities and figure out how things work. They turn to books and experts as needed. Their tests are not standardized multiple-choice tests, but rather the results they have successfully achieved by meeting a real, well-defined challenge.

A common exercise In many engineering schools these days is to give groups of students something such as a raw egg and tell them to select from materials provided a way of packaging the egg so that it can be dropped from four stories onto concrete and not break. The students do not learn to break up the workload into separate sections, but rather they learn to work as a team to *figure out* how to successfully pull off the challenge in this context.

No multiple-choice test is an equally competent measure of success. As any pragmatist would explain, *learning that counts* is seen in the solving of further intellectual challenges and not in any other way.

So, does the pragmatist theory of knowledge have something to offer educational stakeholders at this level of practice? What do you think?

If pragmatism is to help stakeholders make for better education, it has to be built on the heart of pragmatism's theory of knowledge and go forward from there. As you will see later, there is reason to believe that pragmatism can accommodate a few different theories of knowledge that stakeholders in Levels 1 and 3 might have.

It is time to turn to the stakeholders at Level 3. These are the researchers, as opposed to policy-makers or bosses. For want of a better term these will be called *evidentialists*, and they more or less embrace a theory of knowledge by the same name. The next chapter will explain something about this theory of knowledge, and then the following chapter will show how this helps understand more thoroughly the endeavor of educational researchers.

SUMMARY, RECOMMENDATIONS, AND CAVEATS

Summary

1. Genuine pragmatists may find a number of challenges fascinating, but they were always ones where they can construe a clear problem space to be coordinated by a well-articulated purpose.
2. Today's school administrators often feel as if they are living under the sword of Damocles. If school or district standardized test scores do not meet state requirements or board expectations, heads might roll. In addition, inappropriate behavior by teachers toward students or false accusations towards staff can quickly escalate into job termination, while attention to education seems beyond the constellation of immediate problem spaces.
3. Administrators can get things right or wrong. Truth matters. However, the constellation of context-dependent challenges is not hierarchically organized or interconnected in any obvious way. As a consequence, the general purpose of socialization and student building through initiation into the Great Conversation is sometimes difficult to address amid a tangle of seemingly unrelated crises. Many demands on knowl-

edge reserves are immediately pressing, and draw little from the same pool of intellectual resources.
4. All problems are intellectual challenges, but not all intellectual challenges are problems awaiting ready solution. It took 500 years for Indian mathematicians to decide if zero was indeed a number. Mathematicians today still ponder the effect of dividing by zero. Level 2 stakeholders rarely need to address such challenges, and that may affect their attitude toward the Great Conversation.

Recommendations

1. Be mindful of which context and which purpose need to be addressed before grasping toward any ready "solution."
2. Authentic pragmatists in schooling and educational administration should see leadership as moral architecture.
3. Be mindful of Campbell's law: Quantitative social indicators often have corrupting effects.
4. Total Quality Management champion W. E. Deming similarly warns that people will deliver the number they are asked to deliver. Be careful to identify few and right-minded numerical targets, lest all miss the forest for the trees.
5. When engaged in institutional problem-solving, never confuse personal ambition with the ideal of truth-seeking using skills, dispositions, and background knowledge relevant to the institution's challenge.
6. Authentic pragmatists define and redefine context and purpose in light of the shifting sands of reality.

Caveats

1. Inauthentic pragmatists (swaggerists) disparage the idea of truth in favor of their own opinions, needs, and values. Self-proclaimed pragmatism is something to be wary of and not something to celebrate.
2. Cheating on standardized tests can be a problem-solving strategy in that it makes a problem disappear for a time. But in the end it more than likely will lead to far greater problems and destroy any leadership credibility.
3. Blaming others rarely leads to problem resolution. Instead it tends to confound and lead to further problems and bottlenecks.

Chapter Five

Conceptions of Knowledge III

Instrumentalism, Evidentialism, and Social Constructionism

SKETCHING "ISMS," "ISTS," AND OTHER THEORETICAL PROPOSALS

Keep in mind that chapters 1, 3, and 5 are sketches depicting an array of sophisticated distinctions in theories of knowledge. Depending on the reader's background, these sketches may seem over-simplified or perhaps a bit deeper than the reader expected. In either case the point is to acquaint readers with enough of the technical literature that an implicit understanding of each of the three stakeholder groups will emerge.

These theoretical sketches are intended as general rubrics in high relief, sorting each stakeholder theory of knowledge from that of the others. Three issues that are preserved across the board so far are (1) what to do about the concept of truth, (2) what should privilege a set of beliefs as knowledge, and (3) is there any theory that defeats the skeptic's challenge that nothing can be known.

There are many variants of each of the theories and there is simply no way to responsibly sort through foundationalism and correspondence theory with other realism variants, and then the various instrumentalisms and **contextualism** along with other different pragmatisms, or finally to sort out **reliabilism** from evidentialism and a half-dozen variants within each. Indeed, if this is your first foray into theories of knowledge, you may aptly detect overlapping similarities between realism, pragmatism, and the evidentialism described in this chapter.

This should not be surprising, since in any intellectual field pioneers achieve because, as sociologist of science Robert Merton famously proclaimed, each achievement comes about by standing on the shoulders of one's predecessors. And so it is with evidentialists. Evidentialists reflect insights from various realists and, most particularly, pragmatists. But the shoulders they stand on do not end even there. The **mentalist** as opposed to **objectivist** ambitions of social constructionists are reflected in evidentialists' concern about beliefs and other attitudes of mind.

In this chapter, evidentialists are introduced as a sort of mirror image of pragmatism. This gives the reader with a modest understanding of pragmatism a leg up when summarily considering evidentialist thinking near the end of this chapter.

A MIRROR IMAGE, OR MERELY A NEAR REFLECTION?

Pragmatists believe in truth, but they do not think truth can be grasped with certainty. Consequently, they seek to avoid *manifest error* in thinking and action. Error is manifest when it is detectable using currently available investigative resources. And, when urgency prevails, as in the case of religious commitment, William James at least acknowledges that there is a reasonable decision to be made even when all prospects for identifying manifest error have no realistic prospect of being addressed.

Evidentialists, too, believe in truth. But they believe truth is approachable. Indeed, they go so far as to say that evidence which is true increases the likelihood of approaching at least other truths, some perhaps more sweeping (Conee & Feldman, 2004). So truth is within reach for evidentialists, at least in some cases of responsible investigation. And certainly, in the majority of investigatory cases, evidentialists believe information can be legitimately mustered to certify a successful approach to truth (Feldman, 2009).

The case for a mirror image continues in light of pragmatist and evidentialist sensitivity to the skeptic's relentless demand to answer always and everywhere the question, "How do you know something is true?"

Pragmatists, evidentialists, and even realists treasure the question, "How do you know?" as much as any radical skeptic. The difference between radical skeptics and proponents of the other three positions is that those attempt to address the "How do you know?" question in meaningful ways. In contrast, the skeptic runs the risk of contradicting their own claim, if the claim is that in absence of a complete and certain answer to "How do you know?" then knowledge and truth do not exist. But what about the skeptic's claim itself? Is the skeptic certain of its truth? If so, this seems self-contradictory or, at best, a kind of arrogant special pleading along the lines of "there is only this one truth, and it is mine." But if the claim is one the skeptic merely chooses to assert—perhaps for its shock value—then she has given us no reason to think that the claim is true. Either way, extreme skepticism seems a view that can be set aside to get on with the serious business of attempting to Figure Things Out.

Whether the skeptic is caught up in contradiction is of too little interest to address further since the point here about a mirror image rests on pragmatism and evidentialism both acknowledging truth. The pragmatist acknowledges truth as unavoidably sensible because so much error is encountered through careless thinking and planning. There must be a better way, the pragmatist reasons, and the only path away from error must be toward no other error but rather toward truth itself. At the same time, the evidentialist warrants commitment to truth in light of the intense counterintuitiveness that truth does not exist. Truth is about getting things right, and to the evidentialist it is possible to get things *rightly*. Getting things rightly is a bit of an odd way to put things, but this seems to capture evidentialism in its many variants. As Timothy Williamson explains:

> The extreme relativist belief that all beliefs are somehow equally true implies a refusal to take the challenge of other beliefs seriously. In dismissing the possibility that we are right and they are wrong, it also dismisses the possibility that they are right and we are wrong. (Williamson, 2018, p. 116)

Appreciating that evidence should drive truth-seeking is not new. In the eighteenth century, David Hume counseled that, "the wise man . . . proportions his belief to the evidence" (Hume, 1993/1748, p. 73). Accepting truth as part of the world's "furniture" was captured early in the twentieth century with G. E. Moore's assertion that he doesn't need an expert to prove to him that this is his hand he is holding before his face. Could Moore be deluded? Certainly that is possible in some sense. But his point is that it is so unlikely that he is wrong that it is reckless to think that in each such case of plain commonsense knowledge we must be able to disprove such possibilities before we can truly say that we *know* (Moore, 1959; Sosa, 2015).

Timothy Williamson sums up his treatise, *Knowledge and Its Limits,* with the idea that one's *evidence* is what one knows (Williamson, 2000). So what does one know? Williamson explains that, in full opposition to radical skepticism, inquiry must *begin* with common sense about truth-seeking (Williamson, 2018). There is much to be gained in scientific inquiries, in policy formation, and in educational research by asking "How do you know?" There is also much to be lost when the search for understanding is frustrated at the very start by an extreme and arbitrary requirement (Williamson, 2018; Elgin, 2017; Siegel, 2017).

Each variant of evidentialism is unabashed in its criticism of radical skepticism's destructive agenda. In this they are like the pragmatists' dismissal of radical skepticism. Both positions insist that radical skepticism must never be allowed to destroy the search for understanding, even if they differ in some ways about that search. Hence the metaphor of the two views as mirror images.

Above we noted that evidentialism in its mirror image status with regard to pragmatism is about knowing rightly. It was admitted at the time that *knowing rightly* is a rather odd locution. Certainly one cannot *know wrongly*—can one?

Knowing rightly is used here to caution the reader against concluding that evidentialism is some kind of truth litany reading off established propositions from yet another prior litany of bountiful truths. Evidentialism is not so indiscreetly ambitious. Rather, the general argument is that some things seem true enough to warrant further assent to become part of a set of privileged beliefs, beliefs justifiably identified as expressing knowledge of truth. Expanding that set is the goal.

Note that, like other thinkers about knowledge, evidentialists at times misleadingly use the terms *truth* and *knowledge* as if they were synonymous. They are not. Truth is about mapping onto the world what is. Knowledge is about representing truth. The first is a metaphysical ambition. The second is a semantic goal. In short, the founders of evidentialism write as if systematic detection of the elements of reality, along with use of a proper belief-basing apparatus, produces a reliable recovery of nature's truths. So in their article, "Some Virtues of Evidentialism," Feldman and Conee are saying that a person is warranted in privileging some belief as knowledge (doxastic justification) if and only if a coherent set of beliefs is sufficiently connected to lay out a path to truth-entailing knowledge claims. Proper belief-basing can refer to things such as formal logic, mathematical aggregation, and refined statistical management of data (Feldman & Conee, 2005).

There is much that evidentialists, as well as scientists and scholars of every stripe, have written regarding the reliability of our detection of nature's furniture. This book is no place to attempt a theory of perception or an account of various methods for detecting reality. Instead, we will safely assume that the scientists of the world are doing a reliably good job at detecting features of the world to be used as evidence in more grand truth-seeking efforts.

PROPER BELIEF-BASING AND ITS INCREASING EFFECTIVENESS

How to aggregate data and organize properly based inferences is a key component in evidentialism. Attention to properly based inferences justifying evidenced-based conclusions will be the focus of the rest of this chapter. It is well to note at the outset that not all inquiries involve the same processes for properly basing beliefs. For example, the mathematician Eugenia Cheng in her book, *The Art of Logic in an Illogical World*, explains: "The rules of scientific discovery involve experiments, evidence and replicability. The rules of mathematics do not involve any of these things: they involve logical proof. Mathematical truth is established by constructing logical arguments and that is all" (Cheng, 2018, p. 8). It is up to the researcher to employ the appropriate processes adeptly when constructing evidentiary claims based on acquired detections of reality.

Feldman and Conee acknowledge that acquired evidence is always a mental state of some knower. Still, that does not drive all that is acquired into a netherworld of mere subjective belief. Collectively and collaboratively, humans manage much of the world as a result of prudent investigation. Prudence is intolerant of mere subjectivism in science. Neither the scientist or other knowers need acquiesce to skepticism.

The prudent knower privileges **doxastic attitudes** toward belief only when the attitudes surface above the subjective and justification can be shared on similar grounds of detection and reference among a community of knowers. When rising above the merely subjective, properly based beliefs must be wholly and adequately fitting in coherent fashion with the evidence the knower has at the time (Conee & Feldman, 2004, p. 83).

In making this argument, Conee and Feldman seem to be echoing the intuition of Thomas Kuhn and his unabashed "I am a physicist for gosh sakes." Kuhn, like Conee and Feldman, is stipulating in a commonsense fashion that there is a world beyond the fabrications of the human mind. For Kuhn and other physicists (Becker, 2018; Sokal & Bricmont, 1999), that world can be depicted rightly or wrongly. Of course, neither ordinary knowing nor scientific knowledge aims for a simple snapshot of immediate reality. The aim is to produce ever-more generally applicable characterizations of reality that may extend understanding beyond the moment.

The stipulation "Every event has a cause" has a long history. The stipulation will go unchallenged here. The existence of an event documents the existence of one or more causes—or so the story goes. In order to capture a robust image of reality, scientists must go beyond detailing the immediacy of description to bring proximal causes into the picture as well.

Discovering and justifying probabilistic descriptions of nature became an increasingly acceptable ambition among scientists, beginning with Blaise Pascal and later extending through the use of statistics by people like Ludwig Boltzmann. Probability and statistics were increasingly becoming part of the proper basing of scientific judgments (Hacking, 2006; Gigerenzer, 1989).

In particular, Francis Galton, a cousin of Charles Darwin, advanced the application of statistics to well-reasoned accounts of a number of phenomena previously left to intuition and observational estimates. Galton studied the inheritance of heights and arm lengths in humans, along with inherited talent. He was the originator of the **correlation coefficient** and graphical illustrations of **bivariate distributions**, two concepts that are central to social science research.

Once the cow was out of the barn, so to speak, statistical practices surged in their approximating proficiency. For example, Karl Pearson (1900) reworked Galton's correlation coefficiency into the tool used in the social sciences today and bearing his name: Pearson's correlation coefficient, r.

Pearson's correlation coefficient is the **covariance** of two **variables** divided by the product of their **standard deviation**. It is a measure of the **linear correlation** between two variables X and Y. Specifically, it is a value between +1 and -1, with +1 means absolute correlation, 0 means no correlation, and -1 means a negative correlation between the two variables as described. Galton and Pearson were showing associations with a mathematical rigor suitable to responsible scientific investigation. Einstein used Pearson's r when investigating **Brownian motion** (Porter, 1986).

In the twentieth century Sir Ronald Fisher reinvented much of statistics, save for Pearson's r (Box, 1978). Although Fisher's innovations are legion, only two will be mentioned here. The first is Fisher's concept of *tests of significance*. Tests of significance are meant to properly base the pedigree of an assertion following completion of a study. They are used to determine whether or not the **null hypothesis**—the "no real difference" hypothesis—should be rejected and some specified alternative endorsed. Tests of significance are checks against improper basing of inferences (Fisher, 1922a, 1922b, 1925, 1950).

Tests of significance are mathematically contrived to assess the risk of errant evaluations of plausibility. For example, a significance test of .05 properly bases the conclusion that aggregated data of a study is 95 percent *likely* to be accurate and thus informative about the truth of things. Since most distributions of data fall into a **Gaussian curve,** consequences falling above a certain level of deviation are readily identified and serve to caution the prudent management of alleged *evidence.*

The second Fisherian concept that revolutionized statistically driven science is that of the randomized controlled trial (RCT) (Fisher, 1935). RCTs create groupings free of any evident bias, where all relevant extraneous factors that could affect the outcome are "controlled for" by trying to ensure that they affect both the experimental group and the control group equally. The groups are then subjected to different treatment protocols. These different treatment protocols may also be called "interventions," and the results of these interventions in the experimental group are compared to results from the control group that does not receive the intervention during the course of the study. Results differing from the control group can become grounds for a properly based warrant that the intervention was causative. The RCT research design has become what many call the "gold standard" of laboratory science.

Of course, even with these new tools, the nature of the world is not immediately evident—not even to Fisher himself! Fisher did not suffer fools well. Unfortunately, he had difficulty enduring any challenge to his genius. For example, his mantra still echoes throughout all the sciences today: "Correlation is not causation." This is true, and it is also good advice to scientists looking for important associations among effects in the world, but a focus on the mantra by itself can lead to ill-advised evaluations at times.

Sometimes it is impossible to set up a random controlled trial. Even though RCTs are the gold standard of statistically driven research, telling information in the absence of RCT data may still be within researchers' grasp. One such situation is what has come to be called a "natural experiment" because the conditions, while naturally occurring, approximate to a fair degree those conditions that would be established for an RCT. Evidence is about increasing plausibility, about advancing understanding of the truth.

Ascertaining properly based inferencing warrants in the absence of RCTs can still be an advance toward evidence through the careful observation and identification of data and its subsequent management through properly based inferencing. But evidentialists must explain how more modest and less certain advances toward truth can be achieved using a less exacting warrant.

CORRELATION IS NOT CAUSATION, BUT CAN IT EVER BE PROPERLY BASED WARRANT?

A powerful example of this evidentialist dilemma is exemplified in epidemiological studies of smoking and lung cancer and the relentless admonition of Fisher that "correlation is not causation." Fisher's point here is that correlation can never be a properly based warrant for concluding the truth that some event X caused some effect Y. Is Fisher right? Should evidentialists embrace this admonishment as inferential law or as a valuable heuristic where applicable?

In the early twentieth century, carcinomas of the lung were very rare. By mid-century they were increasingly commonplace, along with an upsurge in a number of other ailments such as emphysema, heart disease, and other cancers. In 1900 the per capita rate of smoking in America was about 54 cigarettes per year. That increased to a high point in 1963 when an estimated 4,345 cigarettes were consumed per adult (National Academy of Sciences, 2007, p. 42). The *effects* were unambiguous. Lung cancer had become epidemic in less than a century. The *causes*, well, they were suggestive at best. Only "suggestive at best," you may exclaim? But, everyone knows that cigarettes cause lung cancer! Was there good evidential data and properly based warrant to conclude in the 1950s that cigarette smoking causes cancer of the lung?

Fisher's dictum that mere correlation is not to be confused with causation was much at the center of the dispute. Certainly the correlation was there. So why was that not sufficient warrant for concluding the causative nature of cigarette smoking on lung cancer? Fisher pointed to other correlations that may have been causative for the increase in lung cancer (Stolley, 1991). For example, within the same time frame and proportionately matched to the increase in lung cancer were factors such as increased manufacturing throughout the industrialized world, a dramatic increase in automotive emissions, and the tarring of roads. Fisher insisted each of these factors individually or in concert with one another could be the cause of the increase in lung cancer. So, Fisher's conclusion was that without an account of these other possible **confounders,** smoking and cancer could only be shown to be correlated—and that is not the same as causation. So, how were things to be resolved?

Obviously ethics would not allow researchers to set up an RCT making some nonsmokers smoke and preventing others from beginning. Nonetheless, some studies established statistical correlations that were outlandishly high (Doll & Hill, 1950). It is important to recognize that evidentialists do not insist on absolute proof. Rather, they insist on optimizing the likelihood that an explanation is more plausible than others on grounds of secure data identification and properly based warranting protocols. In contrast, Fisher complained, that for something to count as evidence of some cause-and-effect relation such that X causes Y, it must be shown that the effect Y, could not occur in the absence of X.

So, if evidence alone can suggest a cause-and-effect relationship and if there is no agreement on standards of evidence or how evidence should be mathematically managed, then science is inevitably at loose ends. Consequently, by default, something such as social constructionism or, worse yet, skepticism is all that is left to characterize what really goes on in science. There has to be a way out of this impasse.

If there was no increase in smoking after 1902, how likely is it that lung cancer would increase? To think about this question, it helps to note that not all countries reporting results of increased lung cancer in their populations had manufacturing or road expansion similar to that of the United States. Yet, these countries too seemed to be experiencing an increase in lung cancer in proportion to the popularity of smoking. Is there a way of managing evidence that does not dismiss Fisher's caution out of hand but acknowledges other protocols for properly based warrants?

There is.

Biostatistician Sewall Wright and educational psychologist Barbara Burks proposed an approach that today is called **path analysis** (Wright, 1921; Burks, 1926). In path analysis researchers manage data in light of asking a counterfactual question about data's likely course *if* things had been different in specifically defined ways. A counterfactual question is simply a question that asks, in the absence of the proposed cause X, how likely is it that the effect Y would still have occurred?

Using path analysis as a warrant, scientists countered Fisher's relentless insistence that correlation is not causation. Using path analysis, researchers established that cigarette smoking was indeed a likely and strongly causative agent of lung cancer. An evidential chain relying heavily on Bayesian inverse probabilities of accumulating evidence and eliminating other possible causal agents led the commissions to conclude that smoking causes cancer (Pearl & MacKenzie, 2018).

This use of an alternative to RCT is an exemplar of responsibly acquired knowledge even in the absence of narrowly constrained laboratory protocols. The variety of statistical methodologies that continue to evolve, especially Bayesian strategies and path analysis, supports the evidentialists' ambition to approach truth through properly based warrants and thereby strengthening plausibility of explanation.

Evidentialism is summarily a matter of collecting data, aggregating and arranging it according to properly based warrants of inference. This is done in the hope and reasonable expectation that such justificatory protocols will lead to a closer alignment of plausible explanation with truth. For evidentialists and realists alike, truth is the holy grail of scientific research. It is always and everywhere a proper and unrelenting ideal. But for evidentialists, unlike pragmatists, beyond evidence there are no other warranting grounds for drawing conclusions about reality, no matter how significant or urgent those considerations may seem.

RCTs are designed to separate experimental subjects into randomly selected groups that can be followed from beginning of a trial to the end. Deviations among the groups and from a controlled group receiving no intervention are typically considered revealing of interventional effects. This is still the gold standard in statistical evaluation of interventional results. Properly *evident* deviations in controlled experiments are likely to reveal the world as it is under specific conditions. It is important to note that evidentialism encourages a more robust search for truth than was acceptable under the auspices of statistical pioneers such as Fisher.

SHOULD CAUSATION BE A TARGET OF PROPERLY BASED INFERENCING?

Imagine the world at any moment is comprised of effects and nothing more. Impossible, right? The very concept of effect implies cause. If there are effects that exist at this moment, there must be causes for those effects. Yet the greatest statistician of the past century, R. A. Fisher, was reluctant to make any causal inference based on the data. Here is an important evidentialist point.

The evidentialist is about truth-seeking. The evidentialist seeks approximations that increasingly approximate truth. These approximations are not based solely on observation. The whole point of the Fisher example above is to draw attention to the importance to evidentialists of properly based warrant. The conflict about smoking and cancer was not about the observable data. It was about properly based warrant in managing data to construct a justifiable explanation. Wright's and Burks's path analysis warranting strategies preceded the Fisher cancer debate, but had attracted little attention. Since the 1950s things have changed dramatically in recommendations for the statistical use of data. In addition to path analysis, something called Bayesian statistics has proved to be very potent in planning and decision-making.

Science abounds in conflicting claims, writes Peter Achinstein. Assuming the observations are accurate, the only way to resolve competing claims "depends crucially on what is to count as evidence" (Achinstein, 2019, p. 15). He begins, as most evidentialists do, by giving a Bayesian account of properly based inferencing from observation. This means that "something is evidence if and only if it increases the probability of the hypothesis" (2019, p. 15). Formally, the Bayesian evidentialist's claim is as follows:

$$e \text{ is evidence that } h \text{ is true if and only if } p(h/e) > p(h)$$

The theorem means that something counts as evidence e when it affects the probability of the hypothetical explanation h such that the probability of h being *true* is greater, given the appearance of evidence e [$p(h/e)$], than the initial probability of h by itself [$p(h)$] (Achinstein, 2019). Obviously, this invites attention to causal factors determining effects. That A is correlated with B by itself still does not warrant the assertion that A causes B, but neither does it discredit subsequent search for causal efficacy commensurate with observed correlations.

To understand the claims of this book regarding respective theories of knowledge, you need not know the details of either path analysis or Bayesian statistics to recognize that in inferential statistics in particular, there is an increasing interest in mustering evidence to make the best bet even when the absence of evidence makes no open-and-shut cases. To make the best bet about what can be inferred from a data set, attention must focus on the practice of properly based warrant as the evidentialists insist. For evidentialists, causes—not just correlations—must be considered part of the justifiable repertoire of science.

Science makes predictions about estimated cause-and-effect relationships. The existence of an effect is evidence that one or more causes produce the effect. Identifying an effect ought to increase the likelihood of accurately predicting within a theory a most likely cause. In Bayesian statistics observations are formally ordered to predict further confirming or disconfirming evidence. Reliable, formal ordering succeeds when it does, by postulating the existence of causal operations. This is similarly the reasoning of path analysis advocates.

Inverse Bayesian methodologies are used to seek causes from the facts of observed effect. In either direction, the goal is to move away from error, leaving only evident truth approaching ahead. In path analysis, similarly, the counterfactual question of whether or not the effect would have occurred without the cause is utilized to establish a properly based warrant.

Available evidence is limited. It is always limited regardless of how one does science. Yet evidence, while necessarily limited, may be sufficient for justifiable inferencing. For example, Scott Page of the University of Michigan has shown how, in addition to path analysis and Bayesian and other inferential statistics, the triangulation of different statistical models of a single phenomenon can increase the effectiveness of causal inferencing (Page, 2018). Page is among a number of statistical theorists who are creating new inferential statistics in order to account for data that in the past had too often been regarded as suspect. Advances in properly based inferencing are moving science ahead at least as much as additional observed data.

DOES EVIDENTIALISM ACKNOWLEDGE TRUTH IN CAUSAL REASONING?

Computer scientist David Auerbach writes, "We are cursed to be aware of our poverty of understanding and the gaps between our constructions of the world and the world itself, but we can learn to constrain and quantify our lack of understanding" (Auerbach, 2018, p. 5). Here Auerbach laments both the lack of certainty and celebrates the evidentialist search for truth-approximating understanding. Skills of computational understanding continue to advance. So too must skills of properly based warranting advance.

Statisticians are paid to be skeptics; they are the conscience of science (Pearl & MacKenzie, 2018; Halpern, 2016). For example, Judea Pearl is an Olympian statistician and computer scientist. He also lays claim to being a lay philosopher. The latter claim is easy to make since any statistical theoretician is unavoidably engaged in doing philosophy. Pearl is the father of Bayesian computational analysis. This was a giant leap forward in utilizing computer algorithms to do this type of inferential statistics, so it is most provocative when Pearl claims statisticians are both skeptics and the moral heroes of scientific practice (Pearl & MacKenzie, 2018).

The focus of Pearl's provocation is what this chapter has described throughout as the thrust of evidentialist thinking writ large. For Pearl, the research methodologist is a theory of knowledge advocate. The methodologist is not involved in data collection but in arguments about warranting data-collection procedures and in further warranting data aggregation procedures. Importantly, it is the methodologist, and not the practitioner, who scrutinizes the legitimacy of warrantable claims to know.

Scrutinizing these warranting practices leads to skeptical attention each step along the way while avoiding skepticism about truth in general. The statistician in this sense is the moral hero of science because he keeps researchers mindful of both explicit and implicit assumptions in their theory of knowledge. Getting it as right as one can in the search for truth is the non-negotiable quest for proper science. This requires acknowledgement that causes exist and must be accounted for in a responsible fashion (Halpern, 2016).

JUDEA PEARL, DAVID RUBIN, AND OTHER CHAMPIONS IN THE SEARCH FOR TRUTH IN CAUSAL REASONING

As noted above, Judea Pearl is the acknowledged father of computational Bayesian analysis (Halpern, 2016). Pearl's technical work in computational statistics continues to be used in ever-broader scientific circles, but Pearl is not one to rest on his laurels. He has spent 20 years searching ways for science to give ever-more properly based inferential accounts of the concept of causality.

Pearl began his quest by reading the early work of Sewall Wright on path analysis, but Pearl soon discovered that an educational psychologist, Barbara Burks, independently created the structure of path analysis. Wright focused on biological data and Burks focused on social science data. Pearl speculates that because Burks was a woman, her groundbreaking work remained obscured for decades (Pearl & MacKenzie, 2018). In any case, each of these methodologists had discovered legitimate ways for interpreting evidence causally long before the infamous smoking debate brought all methodologists to the table in one way or another.

Inferential statistics advanced by fits and starts from the 1950s until the present. A major pioneer in this advance was David Rubin. Rubin recognized not only a need for causal accounts to advance the potency of science, but he also introduced statistically formal strategies for acknowledging causes (Rubin, 2005). Pearl saw in Rubin's work the central role of identifying paths capable of treating for confounders and yet accumulating evidence indicating a causal direction (Pearl & MacKenzie, 2018).

Pearl began by figuring that the way to identify paths for investigation rested heavily on the preliminary use of counterfactual questions. Philosophers have discussed the theory of knowledge value of counterfactual reasoning for centuries. And the courts have even formalized counterfactual reasoning for utilizing observations as evidence for some questioned cause, yet, as Pearl believes, in inferential statistics there has been too little attention paid to counterfactual reasoning to exploit its robust potential for explaining causal efficacy (Pearl & MacKenzie, 2018).

Haunted by Fisher's insistence that correlation is not causation, researchers were careful to avoid reference to any causation suggestions, resting instead on increasing levels of association in the presence of a predecessor to the effect of interest. Bayesian analysis in particular made this associationist climb increasingly appealing as inferential statistics became more and more the focus of attention among epidemiologists and educational program evaluators in particular.

Pearl, Rubin, and other causal sympathizers were dissatisfied with what they saw as increasingly convoluted ways of treating data to circumvent making any plausible causal identifications (Cole & Herman, 2002). Through the use of path analysis, mapping counterfactual paths can illuminate the reality of causes. If causes can be identified as plausibly evident, then any good evidentialist should be willing to acknowledge their inclusion in contextualized inferencing. Simply pointing to possible confounders only alarms; it does not prescribe action.

Causal identification that is rigorously warranted does provide grounds for increasing or lessening or even abandoning interventions altogether (Staffel, 2020). As noted above, statistics and research methodology textbooks are not recipe books. They provide guidance for answering "How do you know?" questions as best as researchers can imagine. And, the science of statistics and research methodology continues to advance, as is the case with all of the sciences. Improving strategies for properly based warrants can be expected to vary from textbook recommendations over time. The recipes that are most resilient will endure largely intact. Still, there will be adjustments that in general will tend to improve research methodologists' identification and utilization of data.

SUMMARY, RECOMMENDATIONS, AND CAVEATS

Summary

1. Evidentialists believe in truth, so much so that they create rigorous standards both for observation and for tying the truth of evidence together with the best explanation for subsequent truth claims. For evidentialists, knowledge and truth claims are nearly the same.
2. Evidentialists insist on rigorous rules of inference to justify tying together observations and conclusions. These rules are often statistical and not to be confused with the purity of mathematical probability.
3. Evidentialists are especially concerned with the challenge of authenticating the claims of the sciences.
4. Evidentialists are achievement oriented. That means they focus not on propositional entailment of conclusions, but rather clarity of expression and inference-making that draws the theories of investigators

closer to reality unadulterated by various contaminants such as bias, inaccurate perception, and errors of record.
5. When evaluating programs, evidentialists believe their statistically based comparisons reveal worldly conditions and not merely theoretical speculation or professional opinion.

Recommendations

1. Respect responsibly acquired data. Keep in mind, however, that data can be contaminated and thus can never guarantee certainty.
2. In program evaluation, if the data look too perfect, then suspect contamination.
3. Never close the door on what science might still have to offer regarding learning. The cognitive sciences and neuroscience, for example, are just beginning to identify data that is foundational to understanding learning.
4. If research leads to achievements in better understanding reality, evidentialists endorse the protocols employed. For example, qualitative research can be performed in ways that satisfy evidentialist commitments even though they do not exhibit the formal rigor of the most advanced sciences.

Caveats

1. While evidentialism is about practices and protocols for optimizing the recovery of information about reality, they never eschew the idea of there being a genuine truth.
2. Keep in mind that, no matter how good the research, no truth-seeking efforts can ever guarantee unimpeachable conclusions.
3. Research methodology of any kind is always a branch of philosophy through and through. And, as with any philosophy, there can always emerge reasons for reform and amelioration. For example, in the past 100 years serious advances in and reconsideration of topics such as tests of significance, computational Bayesianism, causative path analysis, and range of confounder identification have all changed as a result of reasoned philosophical argument.

4. A researcher who has forgotten her debt to the philosophical foundations of her methodological strategies has lost her conceptual moorings.

Chapter Six

Educational Researchers as Instrumentalists, Evidentialists, or Social Constructionists

DO STUDENTS ONLY PROBABLY LEARN? DO TEACHERS ONLY PROBABLY TEACH?

As chapter 5 makes clear, educational researchers' approach to the theory of knowledge is evidentialist in general. This means they set out to find what might be true rather than false, might be right rather than wrong, and might be better rather than worse. They are not engaged in trying to make the community of researchers content with shared opinion. Their ambitions are greater. They hope to approach truth in order that others can utilize that knowledge to make things better for stakeholders (Slavin, 2002; Rubin, 2005).

Observation is an important step in truth-seeking. But, as evidentialists generally acknowledge, it is the use of properly based inferencing practices that grounds the identification of evidence and then prescribes drawing warrantable conclusions. Research methodologists are unavoidably drawn into doing philosophy as they advance claims of what should count as proper evidence and well-founded warrants aimed toward a truthful rendering of reality.

Statistical studies are likely approximations of truth, that is, approximate representations of reality. Researchers deliver their conclusions with caveats and a probabilistic summary (Jackson, 2018; Levin, 2012; Wainer, 2009).

Statistical conclusions are the offerings to stakeholders from the level of educational sciences. Their research approximations are meant to reveal when most students experience optimal learning. The statistical conclusions of educational researchers are not so flimsy as to limit themselves to conclusions about what individual students are only probably learning.

Similarly, researcher evaluations of programs, curricular effectiveness, and instructional strategies are not meant to indicate that teachers are probably teaching. Rather, they are meant to indicate when and how teachers demonstrate effective best practices. Effective best practices increase learner opportunities for a genuinely purposeful and robust education.

There is much packed into the two paragraphs immediately above. They note unequivocally the following commitments of practitioner stakeholders in educational research. First, researchers in learning science go to great lengths to fulfill the evidentialist ambition of drawing right-minded conclusions about what students are actually learning both naturally and as a consequence of select interventions.

Second, when investigating teacher and programmatic effectiveness, note that teacher performance and programmatic potency can be measured **objectively**. To the evidentialist, research aims at far more than felicitous, shared agreement among a community of stakeholders. Rather, stakeholders are drawn into shared agreement because the conclusions exhibit a *solid base of reliable evidence*, believable in light of shared expert evaluation.

Third, educational researchers aim beyond the learning sciences alone to investigate educational robustness of programs, curricula, and more. In doing so they are unavoidably drawn into making value judgements. These value judgements are implicit in any context in which best practices are said to be identifiable.

Learning doesn't occur in a vacuum. And much of learning occurs in the absence of teachers. The phrase *best practices* denote comparative judgements that are made about different interventionist practices. The word "best" is obviously a value-laden term. It denotes that some interventionist activities are to be preferred over others. Best practices acknowledge there is value to be sought as well as noting moral restraints on what interventions are to be preferred (Campbell-Whatley et al., 2016; Coburn & Spillane, 2016).

Recognizing and committing to value in interventionist strategies limits the range of acceptable instructional and curricular interventions. Education researchers are interested in more than neuronal activity and the building of synaptic connections. Researchers in the educational sciences have an implicit commitment to *getting right what is worth learning* (Koretz, 2008). Getting right what is worth learning requires imagining a future that preserves the importance of learner autonomy and advances cooperative sophistication that improves the collective dynamic of the educational community.

A consequence of the above is that the educational sciences are shown as naturally bifurcated into learning sciences on the one hand, and program evaluation on the other. Researchers in the learning sciences lean more toward engagement in the pristine world of science. Researchers in program evaluation are frequently brought into dynamic interaction with Level 2 pragmatist stakeholders.

The bifurcation of educational research is not unlike the bifurcation one finds in the biomedical sciences, where research on clinical best practices interacts with but is set apart from scientific work in molecular genetics, biochemistry, and so on. Yet, regardless of apparent bifurcation of interest, the evidentialist thrust in theory of knowledge palpably unifies all.

PROGRAM EVALUATION VERSUS LEARNING SCIENCE

Since program evaluation is probably the first to cross the minds of all three levels of stakeholders when considering matters of education, the nature of program evaluation will be briefly explored first. There is no better place to begin the study of program evaluation in education than with the seminal and visionary work of Michael Scriven. Michael Scriven is a former president of the American Educational Research Association and also a former president of the American Evaluation Association. He is a professionally trained academic philosopher who served as the president of the Pacific Division of the American Philosophical Association. His monograph, *Evaluation Thesaurus*, now in its fourth edition (Scriven, 1991), is a great place for novices to get an introductory overview of program evaluation.

Two words common in educational parlance at every stakeholder level are *assessment* and *evaluation*. To a novice, the two words are often used synonymously. In professional discourse it is imperative to distinguish between the two concepts. Assessment denotes the measurement of observational data. When on a road trip a person may look at her watch and see what time it is. That is an assessment. She may note how many miles she has driven. That too is an assessment. Then what?

The traveler may want to make a judgement about her progress during the road trip. She looks at the assessment data of time passed and distanced travelled. She then evaluates whether or not she is making "good time." If she is advancing to her goal faster than expected, then that is good time. If she is advancing slower than expected, that is bad time. Evaluation is about interpretation of data. And as Scriven points out, evaluation is always undertaken in the context of some set of values (Scriven, 1991).

To help people keep in mind the value-laden nature of evaluation, Scriven recommends noting that the word "evaluation" embeds the root of the word "value." And this, he explains, is how things are in practice. Evaluation unavoidably embeds values when interpreting assessment data.

Individual teachers often take note of student responsiveness to a lesson she teaches one way in comparison to her approach on another. The comparative difference reflects not only measurable differences but also what she values about the learning involved (Yeh, 2001). This inherent value threads through all educational program evaluation, just as Scriven explains.

In a recent issue of the journal *Educational Researcher*, an article compared student performance on an international set of data from the Program for International Student Assessment (PISA), a program coordinated by the Organization for Economic Cooperation and Development (OECD). The article is titled "Comparing the Efficiency of Schools through International Bench-Marking: Results for an Empirical Analysis of OECD PISA 2012 Data" (Agasisti & Zoido, 2018). The title using the term "an empirical analysis" makes it sound like an assessment piece wherein everything is done by the numbers. But this is not so.

The term "efficiency" is inherently a value-laden term. One can assign an **operational definition** to the term, but the definition would give testimony to what is valued in the course of the study. In addition, using PISA assessment data reflects implicit valuing of what PISA is assessing. PISA data is produced in the context of some theory for purposes of research. There is nothing wrong with that, but the fact remains that it is not a value-free assessment (Duncan, 2010).

One can study a topic like the exchange of calcium and sodium ions across cell membranes in a value-free context, but such a pristine and narrow focus is rarely if ever available to educational scientists doing program evaluation (American Statistical Association, 2014). Program evaluation is ultimately about success or failure of some program (Brighouse et al., 2018), and it is important while doing such research to remain mindful of entangling values (Baron & Hershey, 1988).

The consequences of educational intervention would never be responsibly considered if there were not programmatic evaluations to interpret and reflect on (Booher-Jennings, 2005; Coburn & Stein, 2010). Still, this interpretation and reflection is always somewhat value laden. This is not a flaw. In educational program evaluation, the implicit goal is always to make things better, just as is the case in medicine with epidemiological studies. The reason one evaluates an educational program is similar to the reason an epidemiologist studies the range and distribution of disease and characteristic health practices. In the end the goal to make things better for all affected by the relevant causative agents. Note the reference here to causative.

At least since the great smoking debates, researchers in education and epidemiology have acknowledged the need for more relaxed restrictions on the identification of likely causes. If knowledge is to approach truth, then evidence of causation must be allowed and treated gingerly, with respect, just as researchers do with observation. Error is always a present threat in any judgment making, but to shy away from truth-seeking about causes is to abandon the quest for understanding and the opportunity to improve.

Properly based research protocols for causation, such as Burks and Wrights' path analysis, illuminated the smoking debate of the 1950s and are now increasingly central in much educational research into interventionist activity (Freedman, 1987; Rubin, 1974). And, in open evidentialist fashion, probabilistic evidence in general is increasingly welcomed as a source of truth-enhancing knowledge throughout the social sciences (Friedman & Turri, 2015; Blaylock, 1964; Feldman, 1988).

Because of the effects on all three levels of stakeholders, research into program evaluation often attracts the lion's share of attention in teacher preparation and in the eyes of the lay public. Yet, as important as program evaluation is to the scientific purist, work in the learning sciences may be the most exciting.

There is no way to present even a sketch of the scientific work currently illuminating learning. The best one can do is to point out a few markers for the interested reader to pursue further on her own. As good a place to start as any is Robert Sapolsky's recent book *Behave* (Sapolsky, 2018). The first half of the book give an informative survey of the neuroscience behind the brain's learning activity, while the second half of the book explores the effects of culture and evolution on our human learning apparatus.

Think about it. There is no learning that is not accommodated by and does not result in neurophysiological activity. The learning sciences are on the threshold of understanding synaptic growth, epigenetics, and the cascading effects of gene activity. Twenty-two genes have been identified so far that play a role in intelligence. There will likely be more identifications and these all must somehow interact with the formational effects of culture and environment.

Physicist Leonard Mlodinow and psychologist Michael Tomasello, to name just two, have taken on the task of explaining in grand terms the dynamic that accounts for human flexible thinking (Mlodinow, 2018) on the one hand and human abstractions and collaborations emerging from evolutionary history on the other (Tomasello, 2014, 2019). But none of this work leads directly to prescriptions for classroom practice.

On the other hand, taken as a whole, it all helps to lay out the foundation for the Great Conversation of Humankind (Wagner et al., 2016, 2017, 2018; Wagner & Simpson, 2008). Both as individuals and as groups, the physiology of human learning is similar to other animals in many ways, and yet it is vastly different as well.

The learning sciences are not restricted to evolution and physiology. In developmental psychology, Allison Gopnik has demonstrated the awesome hypothesis-testing skills of very young children, even in infancy (Gopnik et al., 1999). She has also shown a developmental path for moral development (Gopnik, 2009, 2016). Gopnik's evidence has explained how old schemes of schooling as indoctrination by rubric fail to take advantage of children's natural epistemic engine.

There is more. As psychologists learn more about the biochemistry of motivation and its social concomitants, distinctions between sympathy and empathy emerge as sources of learning inspiration. Yale psychologist Paul Bloom has acquired evidence indicating that humans are born with a sense of social sympathy, much as David Hume suspected long ago. Moreover, by avoiding mere speculation and adhering to strictures of properly based warranting, Bloom has arrived at conclusions suggesting that while sympathy can be utilized to motivate youngsters to cooperative action, empathy is less predictable and even less valuable as a general sense of moral development as other suppose (Bloom, 2016).

None of these developments in the learning sciences could have been achieved in the absence of probabilistic protocols employed generally in properly based warranting practices in each of the learning sciences. As the learning sciences advance our knowledge, it is more than collective whimsy and capriciousness, as skeptics or social constructionists might insist. This advance represents ever-more secure representations of reality, that is, truth.

IS EVIDENCE NECESSARILY SUBORDINATE TO THE MOST RECENT KNOWLEDGE CLAIMS?

Evidence is related to knowledge claims. And knowledge claims are related to evidentiary claims. Old and new knowledge claims may rest on the same evidence. Revision of warrantable inference may at times be responsible for the evolution of knowledge. Evidentialists are forever vigilant about properly based warranting at every level of data collection, representation, and interpretation because evidentialist researchers are truth-seekers, and they expect knowledge claims to be warrantable only when based in evidence. At heart, evidentialists are skeptical about ever arriving finally at truth. Still, evidentialists are not skeptics! They view truth as real and as approachable.

For evidentialists, knowledge closely aligns with truth in the absence of error. How close the alignment is, one can never know for sure. Through error-avoiding, warrantable strategies, researchers can approximate ever-closer alignment with how things are in truth.

Thomas Kuhn, following Hanson, suggested that all observation is "theory laden"—that is, we do not simply see things and that becomes evidence. In the sciences we must make use of instruments to make our observations (Hanson, 1958; Kuhn, 1970). Some instruments can be simple, like a mercury thermometer, but other instruments can be formidably complex, like an atom smasher at Fermilab. For observations to count as evidence we need to understand how they came to be produced, and that requires either an explicit or implicit theory of the processes that produced them. The influence of theory on observation is why theory can sometimes distort what counts as evidence. Still, there is a difference between sometimes distorting what counts as evidence versus undermining the very existence of evidence.

Evidentialists in the learning sciences and program evaluation must look beyond the most immediately obvious explanation of the evidence they obtain. Their skeptical impulses should lead to getting things right and not merely securing agreement among fellow observers. A case in point follows.

The great champion of behaviorism, B. F. Skinner, taught Nicole Wagner, daughter of one of the authors, a trick for memorizing a speech she had to learn for school. He said, "Run off 25 copies of the speech. Have your father 'white out' three or four words on the first copy, six to eight on the next page, and so on until the last page has only a couple of words left. The words blanked out should be chosen at random for each page."

The trick worked like a charm! Was confirmation of Skinner's recommendation evidence for someone, and thus confirming of some truth? The answer is yes, but not as you may think. Nicole was given a hypothesis and saw it work. For her, the confirmation is evidence of the effectiveness of the "white out" strategy. The truth involved is that she implemented the strategy and did well in her recitation. She was unaware of any defeaters or of any confounding factors that might falsify or distort this conclusion.

Keep in mind what Nicole's evidence was and what it confirmed. The evidence was about her using a trick to complete a very narrowly contrived task. It was not evidence of a standardized protocol. It provided no account of more general application. The sample applied to the truth-seeker's experience of the moment, and not beyond. There was no serious effort to identify either possible confounders or defeaters for the proposed evidential truth. Nicole's evidence was sound as it stood in relation to *her conclusion*, but would her evidence be accepted as indicative of the truth of Skinner's behavioral theory?

Nicole's evidence may be weakly supportive of behavioral theory. But, given the grandness of the theory's claims, no properly based warrants used in psychology would allow such observation to count as strongly evidential of behavioristic truth. Strength of evidential potency is not simply a matter of observational reliability or psychological potency in the mind of an observer. Behaviorism's warrant must rely on firmer grounds. Skinner's recommendation here is perhaps best thought of as an engineering strategy. Engineering strategies are not necessarily accompanied by a coherent set of warrants establishing scientific knowledge.

In the case of behaviorism, Noam Chomsky showed why behaviorism could not muster sufficient evidence to warrant an adequate account for human nature, since human children at a very early age learn to create and understand meaningful sentences that they have not heard before and will not hear again. Thus their behavior lacks the repetition needed for Skinner's operant conditioning via reinforcement to work (Chomsky, 1959). Later cognitive psychologists such as George Miller (2003) went on to show that other approaches to psychology accounted for much that was confounding of behavioristic claims. These and other accounts contradicted behavioristic efforts to account generally for human behavior. As time passed, Alfie Kohn and Barry Schwartz independently assembled research that they claimed provided evidence that a behavioral approach could even be damaging to student learning by substituting an extrinsic reward for the intrinsic satisfaction of coming to understand something new (Kohn, 2018; Schwartz, 1987).

The evidentialist point to be gleaned here is that neither observation of an external reality nor confidence in one's impressions alone strengthen the credibility of warrantable claims to know. Focus on properly based beliefs upheld by a theory of knowledge is unavoidable when doing science.

The learning sciences have been developing in credible fashion over the years, but as in all sciences and intellectual endeavors in general, there are rabbit holes taking travelers far from the journey's goal. Consider the following advance in the learning sciences that is still of interest to educators even though it is from more than half a century ago.

Psychologist Leon Festinger's classic book on cognitive dissonance (1957) set the stage for Festinger and Carlsmith's important cognitive dissonance paper, which gives us an example of evidence identified and managed in light of a properly based warrant (Festinger & Carlsmith, 1959). The paper serves as an excellent example of aligning warrant and observations. The observational data Festinger and Carlsmith were interested in had been of interest to other researchers previously (Janis & King, 1954; Kelman, 1953). It is the subsequent explanation of Festinger and Carlsmith's own and other's data that led to this classic piece being cited nearly 4,000 times over the years.

In this paper, Festinger and Carlsmith acknowledged observational data recovered by others as weakly supportive of their argument and explained why this data could only be considered weakly supportive. This is an example of taking care to present to the reader properly based beliefs. They then described their own efforts at collecting relevant evidence, and how this evidence furnished further support for their conclusions. For example, they gave significant consideration to a possible alternative explanation, which they rejected before concluding that their data "strongly corroborate" two derivations from Festinger's cognitive dissonance theory:

1. If a person is induced to do or say something which is contrary to his private opinion, there will be a tendency for him to change his opinion so as to bring it into correspondence with what he has done or said.

2. The larger the pressure used to elicit the overt behavior (beyond the minimum needed to elicit it), the weaker will be the above-mentioned tendency. (Festinger & Carlsmith, 1959, p. 210)

As a result of this paper, subsequent researchers can legitimately claim to know, based on the available evidence, that people attend more to figuring out an idea when presented with examples of *disconfirming data*. The authors of this book have joined with colleagues exploiting this knowledge for classroom practice in three other books (Wagner et al., 2016, 2017, 2018).

Ever hear people say, "Let the data speak for itself"? Of course, that is an amusing statement inasmuch as there are no talking data. Furthermore, there is no assumption-free data collecting, data aggregation, or interpretation in science or anywhere else in intellectual life.

Festinger and Carlsmith's paper exemplifies, in a pithily written research report, that the researcher's implicit theory of knowledge is fundamental to revealing the heart and legitimacy of specific knowledge claims, experimentally derived or otherwise. Researchers are not social constructionists because the data is not socially constructed. It is not simple agreement that makes data, but rather it is data that can underwrite agreement in the community of researchers.

The rules of inference are more than mere social constructions inasmuch as they are developed with an eye to approaching truth in a broad range of studies and not merely to suit the fancy of the particular researchers engaged at the moment. In short, research is found to be justified in light of acquired data and the independent evolution of prescriptions and prohibitions for inferencing by the relevant truth-seeking community.

CAUSAL REASONING AND A PROPERLY BASED WARRANT IN THE LEARNING SCIENCES

The fact that the learning sciences are so much more advanced than they were, say, 70 or 80 years ago, does not mean that truth changes. Truth does not change. Truth simply is the representation of reality as it is without evident error. Whether or not truth can ever be fully grasped without evident error is a question perhaps for metaphysics, but it is not at issue here.

What beliefs or sets of beliefs deserve to be privileged as suitably justified to count as knowledge is what matters in this chapter. Specific knowledge claims may change over time, but that does not change reality in the absence of human investigation. Moreover, the changes in justified knowledge claims are not capricious or whimsical. The changes are implemented with an eye to a more successful ascent in the approach to truth.

Beliefs of the past retain their privileged status as knowledge to the extent that the evidence to date wholeheartedly supports this status. In the case of the Festinger and Carlsmith paper, the privileged status of their knowledge claims has held up well. In contrast, Skinner's investigation into verbal behavior was seriously challenged on the grounds of defeaters and possible confounders, and it has never recovered (Chomsky, 1959).

Before there were ever schools or colleges of education, educational researchers traced their origins back to statistical innovators in the nineteenth and early twentieth centuries like Francis Galton and Karl Pearson, and shortly thereafter to psychologists such as E. L. Thorndike and Lewis Terman. Educational research as a science is unavoidably in lockstep with developments in statistics (Tyack & Cuban, 1997), but this lockstep does not remove educational science from the need for theorizing and even philosophizing.

Research methodologists continue to advance the cause of properly based warrants, so not long ago, a lively debate surrounding the use of Fisher's tests of significance swept through educational research as it did through the ranks of statistical methodologists. Changes in statistical theory change educational research (McLean & Ernest, 1998).

Theory of knowledge and more generally philosophy of science are evident either implicitly or explicitly in all changes and discussions of change in statistical research methodology. To ignore these developments leads to fundamental misunderstanding of the educational sciences and the methodologies they are dependent upon.

REACHING FOR PLAUSIBLE UNDERSTANDING VERSUS PREACHING FOR PLANNING

Stakeholders in each of the three levels of education would surely agree that they hope to contribute to making education better. For example, parents want students to learn what is what. Teachers want to develop student understanding, critical thinking, autonomy, and general capacity to participate in the Great Conversation of Humankind. Administrators and policy-makers want to create programs that address all of the above along with other dictates of society.

What about this third level of stakeholder? What is it they want to do for education? What can they do for education?

Advise and consent.

Starting from early studies in paper-and-pencil tests for intelligence assessment, the learning sciences today cut across neuroscience and the cognitive sciences, scouting for opportunities created by computational Bayesian analysis, by mathematical game theory, by evolutionary psychology, and by "positive psychology" in addition to old stalwarts such as social and developmental psychology. Add to this list the biomedical sciences, economics, and sociology, and the multiplicity of considerations is staggering.

To give a sense of the magnitude of the challenge, there are more than 3,000 research journals publishing in areas of the learning sciences, and there are open access publications increasing at a seemingly inexhaustible pace. So, the first task of educational researchers committed to the learning sciences is to review and contribute to the growing body of responsibly derived evidence available for theorizing and policy-making.

Beyond the learning sciences, educational researchers are called upon to assess the programs that policy-makers and administrators implement. Certainly here, as in research in the learning sciences, researchers must keep abreast of work in statistical methodology, but on the surface at least program evaluation does not demand the breadth and depth of understanding challenging learning scientists. Why not?

One can argue that the Level 2 stakeholders, policy-makers, and administrators determine programmatic goals and strategies. Educational researchers are called in after the fact to evaluate how well a program is achieving the ambitions that led to its implementation. But are things really that simple?

Remember we suggested above that all stakeholders would agree that they are in education to make it better. But what does it mean to make education better? Is education only of some instrumental value appended to some superior social, economic, or political goal? Or is education an end in itself? Should it be thought of in that way?

Answers to these questions are hard to pin down but have been pursued by philosophers from early in recorded history to John Dewey, Michael Oakeshott, and R. S. Peters in the twentieth century and then to Nel Noddings, Linda Zagzebski, Diane Ravitch, Linda Darling-Hammond, and Harvey Siegel in the twenty-first century. So, unavoidably, educational research must reserve a place for normative studies of philosophers. And there is more.

Program evaluation, as much as research in the learning sciences, is based on properly warrantable beliefs. Consequently, while some researchers argue that the policy-makers dictate program design and researchers are only there to assess interventionist consequences, nonetheless the researchers cannot escape responsibility for the theory of knowledge commitments that govern initial assessment as well as subsequent evaluation.

Under the driving force of evidentialist sympathies, researchers in program evaluation have been caught up in the philosophy of research methodology as much as those in the learning sciences. For example, where once methodologists limited their evaluations to associations among data, the drive to approach truth has led, grudgingly, to methodological considerations of evidence for causality (Bareinboim & Pearl, 2012; Freedman, 2009; Wainer, 2009).

In addition, researchers in program evaluation have often been called upon to support or to criticize the merits of one or another interventionist program in education. Here we have the crux of the program evaluator's advise and consent role. Like it or not, program evaluators are asked to step outside the role of "arm's length" science and to make recommendations based on their aggregation and interpretation of data (Koretz, 2008; Campbell, 1975).

FOCUS ON RESEARCH

The first lesson to be learned at this stakeholder level is that textbooks on statistics and research design are never to be taken as recipe books. As in all areas of science, research methodologies must not be taken as the final and absolute truth. Research methodologies are to advance understanding and the approach to truth in the context of the science to which they apply. They are simply not a "royal road" to truth procurement.

On the other hand, it would be equally imprudent to regard research methodology as no more than social convention. Greeting others is a social convention. Greetings vary from culture to culture, and in contexts within a culture, but research methodology is usually the same from culture to culture. Studies done in Japan or Germany will often employ the same methods that are employed in the United States, and vice-versa. Research methodologies do change, but they change in light of evidence that shows how better to avoid error when drawing conclusions about the reality under consideration.

Educational researchers in the learning sciences intend to detect, with increasing accuracy, how human minds operate. Educational researchers in program evaluation intend to detect variances that result from interventionist efforts and often, as a consequence, to give advice and consent in matters related to the interventions studied.

Education has taken place throughout all of recorded history and, no doubt, long before that. However, the chance for systematic improvement of educational practices was slow and proceeded haphazardly.

As a consequence of the past 150 years of scientific research, education has acquired the opportunity to hasten the advance of educational practices toward the ideals of developing learner autonomy and universal participation of all in the Great Conversation of Humankind. Stakeholders at this level of educational practice are invaluable to the continued advance of shared human understanding. The challenge now is to effectively bring together the three levels of stakeholders.

SUMMARY, RECOMMENDATIONS, AND CAVEATS

Summary

1. Evidentialists in education are Level 3 professionals. These include scientists, some philosophers of science, and other methodological researchers and statisticians. Typically, they are found in research centers or in the minefields of educational program evaluation.
2. Level 3 stakeholders offer invaluable research services to stakeholders at both the other two levels.
3. Though statistical and quantitative evaluation and decision-making seem ubiquitous in all of education, it may surprise the reader to learn that Level 3 stakeholders seldom get to serve in their full capacity. Too often in cases of program evaluation they are pressured into finding quantitative support for policy rather than advising how the data should control the policy. In addition, their role as guiding philosophers of methodological research is often lost in the clamor for educational personnel who can run numbers according to some prefabricated script.
4. Research methodology classes in all areas of education should begin, as do all philosophy classes focused on science and theory of knowledge, with the questions: How do we know (in teaching, learning,

motivation, and educational practices generally) what we think we know? And, secondly, what do we mean by the concepts we are using, and what is their potential for assisting in the quantitative aggregation and assessment of data?

Recommendations

1. Level 3 researchers outside of the most intense research centers may find they have to make the moral choice of putting their career second to honest and robust reporting of unadulterated data and conclusions.
2. Do not mindlessly adopt recipes for either research or program evaluation. Always try to identify and reflect on the utility of hidden assumptions before designing research or evaluative projects.
3. Avoid language that obfuscates findings. Clarity of expression is vital for research and program evaluation to be understood by others.
4. Reach beyond journals focused exclusively on education. Explore related sciences to ensure your research is as robust and as solidly grounded as possible.
5. Periodically do some more philosophy, namely, review what you think the concept of evidence means in your current and proposed work. Sort through tough questions distinguishing strong evidence from weak evidence.
6. Do not demean research protocols simply because it is not your methodological protocol. Empirical research is done employing a variety of strategies and all are different from qualitative or mixed strategies. The job is to increase understanding of reality, not simply to follow a prescribed rubric.
7. Again, do more philosophy. Analyze and reflect on the inferential warrants of your own research and your discipline's current practices. The great advances in research methodology have nearly always been a matter of extending or revising protocols of warrant.

Caveats

1. Keep objective balance. Research and program evaluation should be kept free from ideological and political affiliations.
2. Remember, properly based beliefs and warrants affect each of the following:

a. Rules for collecting observational data
b. Rules for aggregating observational data
c. Rules for identifying assumptions and confounders
d. Rules for assembling a warrantable argument
e. Rules for the precise use of language
f. Flaws in any of the rule sets enumerated above.

3. Avoid the urge to publish small data too quickly. Haste makes waste in research and program evaluation, just as it does elsewhere.
4. No program should be considered too big to fail. Evaluators must be careful not to blur their role with that of the policy advocate.

Chapter Seven

Bringing the Perspectives Together

THE EVOLUTION OF EXPECTATIONS

Confucius, Lao Tzu, Plato, Buddha, and Aristotle were all teachers. Aristotle was Plato's student, and Plato had been a student of Socrates. In short, each were stakeholders in the first and largest level of educational practice. The ancestry of this level of stakeholder is older than even any of these folks from classical antiquity. Teachers, students, parents, family, friends, and neighbors from millennia ago had to be concerned with matters of truth-seeking and cooperative sharing of understanding (Mlodinow, 2015, 2018; Tomasello, 2014, 2019).

The Great Conversation of Humankind may have begun in families and then in tribes, but the commitment to the Conversation, its ambience, and its truth-seeking ambitions is still current today among this level of stakeholder. The realist theory of knowledge most of these stakeholders adopt is outlined in the first chapter of this book. While education is evolving at an ever-more rapid pace, the early commitment to a realist theory of knowledge among these stakeholders remains as resolute as it ever.

While Confucius, Lao Tzu, Plato, and Aristotle, along with more contemporary figures such as Maria Montessori, A. S. Neill, Leo Tolstoy, and Bertrand Russell, each had their own schools, they would hardly count as the sort of administrators found throughout the world in much of professionalized educational administration. In addition, while each of them wrote about education, not one wrote about educational systems or detailed management policies driving large systems today.

Professional policy-makers and professional administrators are recent arrivals in the social history of the Great Conversation. These stakeholders evolved in Darwinian fashion. Homeschooling, or a respected sage, gave way to one- and two-room schoolhouses, and then those schoolhouses eventually gave way to large incorporated school districts employing lawyers, accountants, statisticians, psychologists, and a variety of policy-makers and administrative stakeholders who emerged as locally contrived practices were vanishing (Banks, 1998; Cuban, 2013; Finnigan & Daly, 2014; Farley-Ripple et al., 2018; Grant, 2012).

THE EVOLVING MIND-SET OF A NEW STAKEHOLDER CLASS

The new stakeholders were no longer realists in their ambitions for a theory of knowledge, nor were they single-minded in the quest for an authentic Great Conversation. This is not to say that such things did not matter to them, but, in addition to education, they now had to contend with schooling practices and policies. Schooling practices and policies focus on logistics, budget management, personnel evaluation, accommodation of competing social forces, social engineering and, lastly, providing a safe place conducive to initiation and continued participation in the Great Conversation.

These schooling responsibilities led the new stakeholders to reconsider the nature of knowledge (Harris et al., 2011; Hirst, 1975). Things like arithmetic, the Pythagorean theorem, and the parts of the cell remained uncontroversial bits of knowledge. But knowing what to do in the management of large school systems seemed less reliable and transient at best. In the nineteenth century "Horace Mann laws" were passed to force parents to have their children attend school. Now truancy laws have to be in place to force students to attend school.

Where once children found their own way to school, brought their own lunches, and played in nearby fields, today students are often bused, fed one or more meals a day at school, participate in physical education and a wide variety of sports competing with other schools, and take part in numerous cultural activities.

Where once students were managed by teachers serving as playground supervisors, there are now school police, metal detectors, counselors, and nurses for securing student safety and health (Ravitch, 2020). Despite those things, students appear to be more susceptible to illnesses, apparent distress, and vicious attacks than ever before. With so many more resources and available expertise, how can this be?

Chalkboards, discussions, recitations, penmanship, and bulletin boards once created the ambience of many classrooms. Today, the flickering glow of computers is everywhere. Anxious students and teachers follow unforgiving rubrics aimed at getting past the next standardized test. In the few discussions that occur, students are told there are no right or wrong answers. So, why bother to raise one's hand to participate?

Teenage **existential angst** seems ubiquitous. And professional management seems in disarray in an increasing number of schools and districts (Gillum & Bello, 2011). Addressing this disarray are hundreds, if not thousands of policy-makers and administrators touting skills at problem-solving ready to be employed when challenges arise. With so many skilled problem-solvers, why aren't problems solved more readily, more resiliently, and with less disarray?

Emerging challenges must be addressed through policy and subsequent administrative protocols. What works somewhat today may not serve well classrooms 10 years in the future or 10 miles to the east or west. The sands are constantly shifting beneath the feet of this new class of policy-solving stakeholders. What to do?

Is it really just the case that policy-makers and administrators must get better at knowing how to do their jobs? If so, the challenge seems daunting at best. The common lament or boast of champion problem-solvers depends on fortunes of the moment. A fictionalized pragmatism wherein a Level 2 stakeholder claims, "I am a problem-solver. I do what works best at the moment," is seldom grounds for concluding all is well with a schooling system.

Consider the following misadventure of what can go wrong with overly confident, free-swinging leaders. More than a half-century ago, doctors came up with a drug to relieve nausea in newly pregnant women. It worked like a charm—except when it did not. The drug quelled women's nausea, but an unintended consequence was a number of birth defects. So, was this new drug, thalidomide, a bad idea or a good idea?

Without a moment's hesitation most people conclude it was a bad idea. In hindsight many may also accuse policy-makers of short-sightedness in making the drug available. Is this the end of the story? Is it all just a case of bad policy-making?

Not quite. Not terribly long ago it was discovered that this same drug, thalidomide, is a potent defense for those who have contracted what was once a lethal cancer for which only palliative therapy was prescribed (Stewart, 2014). This old ill-suited drug for nausea in pregnant women is an answer to life extension for many multiple myeloma patients today. Go figure!

Here we have an example of pragmatism in action. The example is not about doing what works best at the time, as some self-proclaimed pragmatists may believe! The example is pragmatic because it is about using the Law of Figuring Things Out to approximate truth by avoiding further error. This law was mentioned earlier and will be discussed in more detail in the next chapter. For now, simply keep in mind that figuring things out is about approximating truth and is not about chance decision-making that just happens to turn out well.

Thalidomide was risky for pregnant women to take, even if it quelled their nausea. That was the truth. It was the truth then, and it is still the truth now. Thalidomide was a promising anti-cancer drug then, as it is now, and that too is a truth. No one knew much about this latter truth until the past 20 years. But each truth existed as a truth—however, not as *known* truths. These beliefs were not privileged at the earlier times of this story. It was not a matter of truth changing, but rather human inability to avoid error in their eagerness to address an immediate problem.

Here is the heart of authentic pragmatism. There is no reason for any policy-maker or administrator to ever give up the ideal of truth. No matter how far out of reach truth may seem at the moment, reality is was it is, and some representations mirror it better than others. An authentic pragmatist sets herself a challenge to address the situation in a way that minimizes evident error.

As much as it serves a realist, truth serves the pragmatist as an ideal. Sorting through proposals that lead to less error than available alternatives is a potent and reasonable practice. Precisely this practice of evaluative review and employing counterfactual reflection makes pragmatists the type of truth-seekers who are more likely to succeed in their professional practice.

Policy-makers and administrators should do their very best evaluating proposals before enacting them. Otherwise, they risk embracing self-defeating, incidental consequences. For Nobel Laureate Daniel Kahneman, this means "slow thinking" one's way through likely errant consequences before taking action (Kahneman, 2011). Slow thinking is a part of the Law of Figuring Things Out. It means taking the time to acknowledge biases, ensure semantic clarity, consider counterfactual causal patterns, and more. Pragmatists cautiously secure their footing and then draw a bead on eliminating distraction from the truth-seeking approximation at hand.

Genuine pragmatists remain ever-alert to signs of flawed evidence, distraction, corruption of observation, and theoretical decay. Pragmatists learn to frame problem sets by securing improved focus on impending issues, all without neglecting unintended consequences lurking just beneath that focus. The goal is to get things more right than ever before and to provide a solution resilient for some time to come.

The confident problem-solver who shoots from the hip is no pragmatist, nor is such a person likely to have a well-thought-out theory of knowledge guiding his or her speculations (Kraut, 1990). As Diane Ravitch summarizes such problem-solver efforts, "these malign efforts come up empty" (Ravitch, 2020, p. 5).

At the present moment in history there are problems, so many problems. In addition, the variety of undeniable problems make it unlikely that shooting from the hip is going to help much. Firing at short range toward increasing, variable, and often indistinct problems blurs the problem-solving focus. Adding resources to bolster a defensive posture against a myriad of suspected and impending dangers affords little benefit over time. For example, installing metal detectors after a school shooting is prudent, but does not solve the problem of local, juvenile violence in either schools or their neighborhoods.

Authentic pragmatists aim at getting things right rather than wrong, better rather than worse. The imitation pragmatists that Ravitch laments seem willing to settle for anything that makes a problem vanish for the moment or distracts from unwanted attention prompted by an impending challenge.

Genuinely pragmatic stakeholders share with other stakeholders a sense of collaborative purpose to serve and protect the Great Conversation. This shared ideal and respect for professional collaborators as well as for the Great Conversation itself brings productive focus to all. In addition, such respect and shared ideals across stakeholder populations tempers disparate and unrealistic ambitions while fostering humility in the face of genuine challenges.

Problem-solving in education must bring Level 1 and Level 3 stakeholders to the table in order for Level 2 stakeholders to initiate prudent and responsible practices across all managed systems.

The principle intellectual tool for pragmatists as well as the other stakeholders is collectively utilizing the Law of Figuring Things Out. The Law of Figuring Things Out is perhaps the most central practice and motivational commitment within the Great Conversation itself. The Law of Figuring Things Out nurtures each participant's theory of knowledge and furthers the quest for shared understanding. From boardrooms to classrooms, all stakeholders must work together to figure out what best sustains the Great Conversation.

Not just any hunch about what to do next will sustain the new megasystem approach to schooling. The larger systems become, the more dangerous shooting-from-the-hip problem-solving becomes. Similarly, obfuscating impending challenges is no substitute for leadership charged with avoiding impending mishaps now as well as in the foreseeable future.

An apt understanding of pragmatism should enable Level 2 stakeholders to see past social forces that might subordinate the ideals of an educational system in a bid for social or political power. The shifting sands of sociopolitical context surrounding a nation's schools should never disrupt administrator commitment to the most general purpose of education, namely, inviting participation in the Great Conversation. This participation is to further develop personal autonomy of students and never to reduce them to systematic subordination by society's power vectors.

One might profitably imagine Level 2 stakeholders as captains of their respective ships. These captains of schooling recognize a common destiny. The destiny is not geographical as it is for ship captains. Instead, these captains of school seek calm waters favorable to education, moment by moment. The seas may be turbulent, but the captain's mindfulness of a final destiny should never be subject to whimsy or to chance. They are charged with seeking an ambience supportive of education and not mere socialization.

To the extent that policy-makers and administrators cater to the wishes of those who hold great power, attention to the development of student personal autonomy may be diverted. The destiny of schooling is to encourage an education that advances personal autonomy and willingness to cooperate with others in as many ways as is imaginably beneficial to all.

Level 2 stakeholders are responsible for balancing all stakeholder educational ambitions. In mathematical game theory and economics it is fashionable to talk about the Pareto frontier. The Pareto frontier is an imaginary set of arrangements of all participants in a system, and the arrangements are such that any change will lead to less benefit for some participant.

Of course, in education, given the disparate social forces involved, the location of the Pareto frontier is often hazy and hard to discern. But, like the ideal of truth, it serves an important motivating function. It sets destiny equally well for all participants. Level 2 stakeholders had to evolve a somewhat different theory of knowledge from that of teachers and schoolmasters past if they are to be in a position to draw from other stakeholders and move toward a point on the Pareto frontier that embraces student building throughout the Great Conversation.

It is no accident that pragmatism took hold among Level 2 stakeholders as it did. Level 2 stakeholders are no more important in fulfilling educational destiny than stakeholders at the other levels, but as the leaders, managers, and policy-makers they especially are charged in bringing all together.

Level 2 stakeholders now must learn to *think more like engineers, rather than as researchers such as philosophers and scientists or as teachers transmitting alleged truth and leading others to think critically.* Engineering practices prove their mettle by showing they work in context.

LEVEL 3 STAKEHOLDERS EMERGE

Alas, context changes. Consequently, the need for better science on which to base subsequent engineering practices is crucial. This need for scientific data through times of change is largely what drove the evolution of Level 3 stakeholders. In the nineteenth century there was some dabbling in the study of learning potential. Sir Francis Galton looked to inheritance traits, Alfred Binet studied problem-solving deficiencies in some students, and Louis Necker studied universals of optical illusion. This was all a bit of fiddling around when compared to today's educational sciences.

Level 2 stakeholders realized they were standing in soft sands. And while someone like Aristotle may have described the greatest ambitions of education with keen insight, he had little to offer the Level 2 practitioner of the twentieth century running large megaschool systems. The twentieth century set the stage for the emergence of Level 3 stakeholders.

To find ways to more systematically increase learning, there needed to be more scientific study of the various learnings possible and their accompanying challenges. To focus more clearly on what is worth learning, there had to be more focus on the philosophy of science and research methodologies in general. And to situate the new learning in local, state, and national contexts that control the funding for public education, there had to evolve sophisticated and respected researchers, namely, those who now comprise Level 3 stakeholders.

With the dawn of the twentieth century, probability theory and statistical strategies for studying all that exists blossomed in every science, and created fields of science where before none existed, such as epidemiology, industrial psychology and, yes, educational sciences as well. Probabilistic evaluations were needed to add clarity to judgments that previously were only intuited or estimated.

The focus on probabilistic tools and statistical philosophy gave greater precision to the concept of evidence than ever before. The better the identifiable evidence, the greater the utility of resulting conclusions. The identification, collection, and statistical management of data led to the evidentialist conviction that properly based beliefs are a consequence of properly managed inferences.

As noted in the previous chapter, data does not speak—ever! Data is always interpreted. The key to turning data into evidence is accurately managing properly based beliefs about systematic observation, about data collection, and about aggregation and organizing, all to render meaningful interpretations. As chapter 5 makes clear, rigor of inferencing is at least as important if not more so than rigor of observation. The educational researcher makes available to Level 2 stakeholders likely strategies for engineering success.

So, can the different stakeholder groups align, or must they forever compete in their ambitions and practices since each relies on a different understanding of knowledge? The three levels of stakeholders can cooperate. Even while working under differing theories of knowledge, their shared respect for the enterprise of the Great Conversation draws them into recognizing differences in expectation and justificatory reasoning while accommodating shared progress supporting a common destiny.

JUSTIFIABLE LEVEL 1 EXPECTATIONS

Level 1 stakeholders as realists are committed to the search for truth. Consequently, their advocates are especially vulnerable to criticisms from skeptics. How, skeptics demand, do Level 1 stakeholders *actually know* if and when they have captured a bit of truth to share? Are not Level 1 stakeholders a bit like the dog forever chasing its own tail with no success?

As long as the concept of truth is treated as something inside the human brain, there is no common ground to build on. Things that occur inside of brains are subject to inexhaustible turbulence. Immune and respiratory disorders, social anxieties, genetic inheritance, cultural pressures of all imaginable kinds, nutrition, guessing strategies, emotions of all sorts, and even changes in the weather, all affect mental life. The skeptic's criticism seems to have some sting. To remove some of this sting it must be remembered, as discussed in chapter 1, that truth and knowledge are two different things. Truth is any representation that maps onto the world as the world is in reality, without any evident error. Knowledge aims at truth, but it is not itself truth.

Remember that we suggested that a logician of the last century offers some help here. Alfred Tarski offered a simple example about truth in the material world: "Snow is white" is true if and only if snow *is* white (Tarski, 1944). If it turns out that snow is not always white, then the sentence is in error and not a truth. Most important, Tarski's example illustrates the idea that truth and knowledge are separate and yet can accommodate the relation of truth and knowledge to each other.

We can never examine all the snow that ever has or will fall. We can try to anticipate every condition that might have an effect on the color of snow. But, the best we can *know* is what we gather from our observations and subsequent thinking about the matter of snow's color. Someone, given much experience, may reasonably claim to know that all snow is white. But surely listeners understand that, as with all knowledge claims, the claim may not be co-extensive with truth itself.

Level 1 stakeholders are like the physicist Thomas Kuhn; they do not doubt that there is a world about which one can be right or wrong, nearly right or nearly wrong, and that this world is independent of all those judgments. For these stakeholders, knowledge that captures truth would be a real gem. But capturing truth need not be the criterion for evaluating all knowledge claims, even for the realist. Knowledge that *appears* unimpeachable deserves privileged treatment among all other beliefs. It is that simple (Mladenovic, 2017).

Both Plato and Aristotle seemed to recognize the importance of this challenge. Each is credited with saying something along the lines of: Truth is a matter of saying what is, that it is, and of saying what is not, that it is not. Philosophers vary on what they take the ancients to mean by such rhetoric. For current purposes, keep it simple. "Saying" is a matter of representing, is it not?

Treat truth as an *ideal* representation of reality and not as a state of mind. One can believe rightly or wrongly how to sum 2 + 2. Assuming $2 + 2 = 4$ is a truth about the world of numbers, the representation is, as an idea, true regardless of where it appears. It is true when written, typed, spoken, or when not portrayed at all. Yet beyond the pristine world of mathematics realists recognize knowledge claims can be challenged and pay their way only to the extent they can resist unjustified criticism. In the end, realists expect to find ever-closer approximations of truth as skill, experience, and chance continue to favor the serious truth-seeker.

JUSTIFIABLE LEVEL 2 EXPECTATIONS

Like Level 1 stakeholders, the pragmatists of Level 2 recognize the meaningfulness of the concept of truth. Truth nails it! Unfortunately, human thinking can never guarantee truth beyond simple mathematics. Consequently, to go about the business of living, deciding, acting, and so on, Level 2 pragmatists need an angle on truth that does not commit them to relentless investigation. Mindful conclusions must direct behavior in the foreseeable future.

In the absence of any guarantee that truth might be captured, the goal is to avoid error in light of human purposes in a given decision-making context (Elgin, 2017). Pragmatists place a premium on *timeliness* much as they do on accuracy (Putnam, 2002, 2009). Guidance is key, perhaps more so than the realist's unrelenting desire for insight. The pragmatic theory of knowledge as portrayed here is about purpose-fulfilling strategies for engaging some aspect of the world.

If there was a slogan to capture what is prized at this level, it might be the lyric of a Pat Benatar song from years ago, "Hit me with your best shot." Pragmatists expect clear focus on context and purpose along with meticulous skills of thinking that will, more often than not, lead away from avoidable error.

JUSTIFIABLE LEVEL 3 EXPECTATIONS

Finally, the evidentialists of Level 3 remain prudently cautious about truth claims (Conee, 2004; Conee & Feldman, 2011). Like the other stakeholders in Level 1 and Level 2, evidentialists do not deny the existence of truth in principle. And, like advocates of Level 2 pragmatism and even some Level 1 realists, evidentialists shy away from taking on the challenge of discussing the metaphysics of truth. More often than not, when they do address truth it shortly becomes clear they are intending to address what others, and the authors of this book, call knowledge.

Knowledge for evidentialists is a set of privileged beliefs that most closely mirror reality compared to any competing beliefs. These privileged beliefs are best grounded, of course, when based on evidence that is true. Surely reasoning from truth ups the odds that one might capture further truth as a result. But prior truth-based knowledge is rarely at hand. As the skeptic might point out, delusions, illusions, and hallucinations are always possible disruptions of accurate belief assessment.

The skeptic's wariness is embraced to a degree by evidentialists, who readily admit truth-seeking should always be accompanied by skepticism. However, a thoroughgoing skepticism is beyond boring—it is a threat to individuals and even to the survival of the species. As a practical matter, survival depends on decision-making and subsequent action. Survival is optimally ensured to the extent that accurate knowledge is obtained and prudently managed. In the modern era, statistical thinking, in particular, has brought both modesty and grounds for confidence to the fore.

Statistical thinking acknowledges upfront that, as Blaise Pascal discovered long ago, most important decisions must be undertaken in conditions of some uncertainty (Hacking, 2006). While a person may not know a particular fact for certain, that doesn't mean that all must be left to a cloud of ignorance. Given the tools of probability, statistical philosophy has evolved research methodologies revealing how some conclusions might be more likely under the circumstances or over the long run than others (Gigerenzer, 1989, 2008).

Today virtually every science avails itself of statistical thinking to justify confidence in some beliefs over demonstrably less favored ones. Scientists are less likely to claim to know the truth of some proposition compared to scientists more than a millennium ago. And today's scientists also have reason to be more assured that their most favored beliefs come closer to the mark than merely relying on the intuitions of smart people as was the case millennia ago.

Evidence, and the conclusions it leads us to, are established through adherence to rigorous procedures of observation, data aggregation, and well-managed inferencing. Together they warrant the privileged status of favored beliefs. To grasp how important this protocol is to evidentialists, consider the following example.

Imagine preparing a class of sixth graders for an exercise in critical thinking. One student, call him Johnny, seems never to pay attention. Midway through your presentation you are convinced that Johnny has not paid attention. To catch him, you ask him to define a word you never used just to see what he might say.

Johnny!

Yes?

What does it mean to ratiocinate?

It means to reason specifically by means of logic.

You are stunned by Johnny's response. How could he know? In the old days of schooling practices teachers were once taught that if a student can define a word and use it in a sentence then the student knows the meaning of the word. Fortunately, education has advanced far beyond that old schooling practice.

Imagine when you called on Johnny he had indeed been daydreaming. He had no idea what you were talking about. Johnny heard his name called and just blurted out something to be funny. Etched on his desk by some other student long ago was the phrase "reason specifically by means of logic." Johnny just slapped together the introduction "It means to . . ." with the etching he read. He expected a big laugh. He did indeed produce the right answer to your question, but he had no idea that it was right or why it might be right. He spoke the truth, but that truth was *unknown* by him.

Evidentialists are savvy about situations like Johnny's. They recognize that knowledge that satisfies the truth-seeking effort must result in conclusions that are justifiable. A lucky guess may turn out to be correct, but it can never be a justifiable conclusion. In certain contexts a lucky guess may be all a person has to go on. But still, a lucky guess is no more than just that. It is never a justified decision warranted by evidence and strict attention to inferencing.

In general, evidentialists are committed to the idea that the concept of truth is an ideal that beckons investigators forward. Most researchers in the educational sciences share this evidentialist conviction. They modestly accept that truth may not be within grasp, just as they grow more confident in the results of well-managed scientific experiments and program evaluations.

Evidentialists acknowledge that research can lead to profoundly wrong conclusions. The primary way for avoiding such calamity is to secure conclusions by referencing well-established evidence, suitably managed by rigorous application of inferential warrants. This is the process of justification. By adhering to rigorous standards of justification, the credibility of Level 3 researchers is sustained and responsibly utilized by stakeholders in the other levels.

Other Level 3 evidentialists such as philosophers of science, statisticians, and research methodologists are always at work developing increasingly more rigorous accounts of inferential warrant (Pearl & MacKenzie, 2018). In the end, evidentialists expect that their investigations will progressively lead to ever-closer approximations of truth.

RESPONSIBLE MODESTY IN RESEARCH AND THEORY

No one is in a position to proclaim to all the world much in the way of grand truth in educational practice. But that does not mean that truth and coordinate theories of knowledge do not play fundamental roles in the development of successful educational practices. In fact, as should be clear, a theory of knowledge that leads us to privilege some beliefs is a driving force at every level of educational practice.

No stakeholder is fine with the idea that their thinking about education or how to go about it is all wrong. There may be intra-level stakeholder disagreements about what counts as knowledge and inter-level stakeholder disagreements about what counts as knowledge as well. But such disagreements need not grind productive educational practice to a halt.

Some parents and some teachers may be in disagreement with others on whether or not evolution, intelligent design or, creationism should be taught as truths or even legitimate candidates for truth. Does the existence of such disagreement count as evidence that the search for truth is pointless, or that there is no truth, or that everyone has their own truths? Not at all. Each of these stakeholders is presumably searching for truth. And presumably, if they are genuine truth-seekers, they do not ignore what others have to say. Why not? Because they are truth-seekers.

What truths should be embraced?

Only genuine truth should be embraced. But given that truth may be out of reach, then knowledge that seems free of evident error ought to hold sway (Dewey, 1908). Finding knowledge claims free of evident error is no easy challenge. Yet it is often doable. For example, there is little doubt about the reality of the technique of carbon dating for telling how long ago a prehistoric village was built or how old a Neanderthal bone is. To cast carbon dating aside would be tantamount to discarding all of physics. Carbon dating makes it clear that the universe is more than 6,000 years old, and much more.

Intra-level discussion of what truths should be included in the curriculum to respectfully accommodate all Level 1 stakeholders is a challenge. But an earnest commitment on all sides to center the curriculum on the best established knowledge is strategically and morally the most responsible route for all to pursue. Does this mean that controversial matters should never be considered?

Nel Noddings, an early champion of feminist ethics and one of a handful of the greatest leaders in education today, wrote a book titled *Educating for Intelligent Belief or Unbelief* (1994). Noddings argues that, skillfully managed by properly trained teachers, discussions of politics and even religion can and should be treated as teachable moments for critical thinking in public high schools. Whether one agrees with Noddings or not, the point is that what knowledge claims Level 1 stakeholders embrace is not nearly as important as their commitment to a theory of knowledge that *aims* at truth.

Disagreements between Level 1 and Level 2 stakeholders will also arise as local sentiments prefer school priorities that are different from those imposed on Level 2 administrators by state or federal regulations (Nichols & Sheffield, 2014). Is there a truth of the proper balance in the case of all such disagreements?

Perhaps. But as Charles Peirce warned, we are unlikely to recognize significant truths even when our knowledge claims hit the mark dead on (Ayer, 1968). Instead, the most that can be achieved is that when disagreements occur, policy-makers and administrators should try to frame the dispute accurately, to scrutinize the evidence thoroughly before drawing any conclusion, and then, as Kahnemann asserts, slow think to a plausible conclusion that is most free of evident error (Kahnemann, 2011).

Credible knowledge claims are mediated to some extent by the theory of knowledge employed by respective stakeholders, and thus there will be variations in what knowledge claims are made. However, since every stakeholder is in the end truth-seeking, being at variance at times can be manageable across stakeholder levels. To anchor knowledge claims across contrasting theories of knowledge, *truth* must be defined as something beyond brain function. Truth among all stakeholder levels must be seen as something that stands apart from the turbulence of human minds (Weinrich, 2014; Williamson, 2018, 2000). Truth must be seen as something other than just one more mental event such as mere belief, doubt, knowledge, suspicion, joy, sadness, and so on. Truth must be recognized as beyond mental life, as a herald beckoning attention from truth-seeking minds.

RESPONSIBLE SYSTEMS OF ACCOUNTABILITY

Finally, classroom teachers' and parents' insistence that students be taught nothing but the facts may run counter to administrators' emphasis on test preparation that proceeds regardless of the ebb and flow of acknowledged facts. Teachers and parents may eschew the researchers' view of research protocols being given preference over what appear to be well-established practices of instruction and curricular content. While researchers worry about such things as confounders, parents and teachers are often simply confounded by researcher worries. So, what standards of accountability should apply, and at what level?

Administrators too are under pressure often imposed by politicians and journalists from outside the institution. Within the institution, administrators may have to confront the fuzzy-headed intellectual concerns of teachers, parents, and some of the most earnest students. These folks want time to question, to doubt, and to reflect on alleged truth claims, including some that are most closely aligned with impending standardized tests. The administrator may fear she is held to accountability standards that leave little room for such intellectualizing.

Fortunately, all is not lost. Once the three levels of educational stakeholders become more alert to the theories of knowledge driving dispositions and instincts from different perspectives, respect for both the differences and the strategies for negotiating among competing theories can lead to new and successful collaborations.

THEORY OF KNOWLEDGE AS THE UNIFYING ENGINE OF RESPONSIBLE AND RESPONSIVE EDUCATION

These theories of knowledge are not incompatible. However, to the extent that stakeholders in education are unaware of the distinct existence of these separate theories, there is a danger that cooperative and collaborate efforts to improve education will be thwarted.

It is easy to imagine how disparities in theories of knowledge can lead to incompatible strategies among the three levels of stakeholder activity. For example, an administrative team working under performance standards imposed by some governing body can see their task as producing the numbers by which they are to be judged. If researchers point to conditions that may limit student inquisitiveness but that are more than likely to improve scores on a standardized test, administrators may ignore the warning of nit-picking researchers.

The place to begin bringing stakeholders together is where there is the most common ground. In this case, that ground for each theory of knowledge is the commitment to discovering truth. By now the reader should already anticipate that the concept of truth employed in these different theories of knowledge is not one that is a feature of individual or even collective mental life.

Knowledge aims at truthful representation. It can do no more. However, that does not discredit the utility of beliefs we credit as knowledge or the value of representations that are approximately truthful. Truth is an ideal.

Acknowledging that truth is the *aim* of knowledge is instructive. When one hopes to bridge the ambitions of the respective and legitimate stakeholders, the theories of knowledge implicitly embedded in the three levels of stakeholder must be recognized as foundational. The idea of grasping truth itself, as opposed to securing knowledge, must be left to metaphysicians. Truth-*securing* is not a productive pursuit for professionals in educational practice. Extending professional understanding and knowledge is required for improvement of institutional services and nurturing the Conversation.

Stakeholders in education are not in the business of denying truth or writing it off as nothing more than historical, geographic, or cultural accident. Yet when confronting the challenges of nailing down truth approximation or lapsing into nihilistic skepticism, the major stakeholder groups have often wandered apart from each other in their apparent theory of knowledge-dependent practices. The way to avoid this disassembling of shared commitment is to get clear about truth as the aim rather than the secured content of knowledge.

Once the concept of truth is recognized as an ideal, then embracing multicultural conventions, individual ambitions, and a legitimate focus on a life well lived become evident both in operational efficiency and in the content of instruction. With the ideal of truth-seeking in hand by all, shared focus accommodating stakeholder uniqueness is more likely to be assured.

When truth is recognized as an ideal and not as a standard of achievement performed by individual minds, the collaborative mission to build students who seek truth by avoiding discernible error is within reach. To seek truth and avoid error is the meta-theory of each of the theories of knowledge discussed above. No teacher, parent, student, administrator, policy-maker, or educational researcher should eschew truth or efforts to build students who are truth-seekers for life.

SUMMARY, RECOMMENDATIONS, AND CAVEATS

Summary

1. Unlike political ideologies wherein true believers seem unable to agree on anything, theorists of knowledge can be accommodating of one another. At least in education, all three levels of stakeholder generally find the concept of truth indispensable. This accommodation, along with shared commitment to student building, ensures grounds for shared purpose despite the absence of a shared canon.
2. Truth-seeking in education in central to the expectations of all stakeholders in education.
3. Student building is perhaps the most central moral commitment in each stakeholder community in education.
4. Student building requires participation in the Great Conversation of Humankind. In turn, the Great Conversation builds on student building to advance the Great Conversation's truth-seeking ventures.
5. The Law of Figuring Things Out is naturally superimposed on each of the theories of knowledge referred to in this book. The more evident this superimposition becomes to stakeholder groups, the more effectively collaboration can advance.
6. The Law of Figuring Things Out is essential for fulfilling stakeholder expectations just as it is central for developing young minds by extending their natural inclinations and capacities for learning into abilities mastered autonomously by each student.

Recommendations

1. Acknowledge that each level of stakeholder is in the truth-seeking business by helping advance the knowledge desired by respective stakeholder groups.
2. Put the questions: "What is meant by the term _____?" and "How does one go about knowing _____?" at the beginning and near the finish of

every professional deliberation and operational planning. In addition, make each question the centerpiece of every teachable moment.
3. As Pascal warned, most decisions are made under conditions of uncertainty. This is true for all education stakeholders and in student building more generally. A focus on the management of evidence and inferential protocols is necessary for fulfilling thoughtful expectations of professionals and students alike.
4. Never focus on making problems "disappear." At whatever stakeholder level, your role is not that of magician. Focus on solving problems and not hiding problems. Use the Law of Figuring Things Out to make things better.
5. Each stakeholder group is unavoidably and fully engaged in managing moral consequences that affect others. Stakeholders must hold themselves responsible for intended and unintended consequences.

Caveats

1. No stakeholder group can afford to operate as an island and fulfill their expectations for education. They cannot succeed independently. They must cooperate and collaborate with one another.
2. Doubt much, but never sacrifice the search for truth.
3. Focus understanding on other stakeholders' expectations while figuring out how to complete this or that task within the proper authority of one's own stakeholder realm or value and expertise.

Chapter Eight

Sketching a Path Forward

AN EVOLUTIONARY SKETCH OF STAKEHOLDERS

The largest and oldest base of educational stakeholders are those who hold an allegiance, implicitly at least, to a realist theory of knowledge. But the world changes, and so what is knowable changes as well. As Michael Tomasello explains, "Natural selection can operate directly only on the way organisms interact with the environment overtly" (Tomasello, 2019, p. 39). So it is that education evolved two additional levels of stakeholders, and each of these came with a new theory of knowledge.

In the nineteenth century, a second level of stakeholders evolved. These were professional administrators and system policy-makers. Early twentieth-century policy-makers in particular were often pragmatists in their theory of knowledge, and they led the emergence of progressive education as a movement. The point of progressive education was on individual problem-solving and skills for addressing immediate challenges.

Later, educational pragmatists were increasingly evident in the ranks of administrators managing the schooling operation of large educational systems. Students needed to be fed and kept secure, intermural competitions were expanding, and the buses needed to run on time.

Educational pragmatists reject the idea that there is a standard set of knowledge claims every student must know (Garrison et al., 2002). They also believe that schooling management requires strategies different from those that had previously sufficed in the nation's more rural days. From logistical issues, budgets, transportation, and intermural competitions to litigation, the urban systems created an evolutionary niche requiring novel adaptations for institutional stability (Peters & Ghiraldelli, 2001).

At about the same time or shortly thereafter, the breadth of science expanded beyond physics and chemistry to biology, geology, and then to a spectrum of social sciences. University departments reflected this evolution transparently. For example, the University of Chicago at the turn of the century had one department named Philosophy, Pedagogy, and Psychology and a second named Political Economy. In less than 30 years, the first department split to become three departments: philosophy, pedagogy, and psychology. Similarly, the second department became three departments as well: political science, sociology, and economics. The application of probability turned social studies into sciences with statistical practices as their basic research methodology.

A few researchers such as Alfred Binet had begun mathematizing educational research. But it was psychologist Lewis Terman's statistical skills that grounded the psychometrics of intelligence test construction. Today the Stanford/Binet IQ test continues to be immensely popular among researchers. E. L. Thorndike (1912) and especially L. L. Thurstone (1925, 1934) were among the most notable pioneers in the new educational sciences.

The new sciences increasingly limited knowledge claims to those exhibiting quantifiable support (Wright, 1921). Statistician Steven Osterlind sums up this evolution of theory of knowledge as follows: "The 130 years or so in which our story [the mathematization of knowledge] occurs are generally acknowledged to be the most productive in human history, eclipsing all others up to then" (Osterlind, 2019, p. 4). The ground for evidentialism was thus seeded.

Herein lies the evolution of the most recent level of education stakeholders. Osterlind recently elaborated: "For the first time in history, using the methods of probability theory, we can anticipate an outcome for almost any event or phenomenon. For all kinds of things, we can describe odds and the likelihood of occurrence. By calculating correlational relationships, we can understand much better how things go together" (Osterlind, 2019, p. 2).

As the century advanced, the competence and notoriety of experimental educational scientists advanced as well (Bloom, 2005; Cronbach & Snow, 1981; Gopnik et al., 2015; Humphrey, 1924; Inhelder & Piaget, 1958; Osterlind, 2010; Piaget, 1954; Skinner, 1938). In addition, statisticians (Rutkowski & Rutkowski, 2016), research methodologists (Blaylock, 1964; Friedman & Turri, 2015; Kelcey et al., 2017; Kleinke, 2017; Koretz, 2005, 2008, 2015,

2017; Rubin, 1976, 1981; Wright, 1983), and even a new breed of educational philosopher, namely, philosophers of science (Norris, 1989; Suppes, 1970) comprised the newly evolved stakeholders.

Advancing developments in probability theory along with increasing attention to properly warranted beliefs (statistics) turned previous intuitive pedagogical studies into little more than a background for Osterlind's quantificational science. Still, as Norwood Hanson explained, no observations are theory free (Hanson, 1958). Background assumptions should still be addressed in even the most advanced education sciences (Harris & Herrington, 2006; King, 2017; Wolgemuth et al., 2017).

No level of stakeholder properly takes priority over the others. The evolution of educational expertise is far from finished. No stakeholders should be overlooked. Each continues to play either an informative or guiding role as massive state and federal systems of education lumber forward. And, contrary to the thrust of Osterlind's account, quantification adds to, but does not discredit, continuing contributions of Level 1 and Level 2 stakeholders.

ARE THE STAKEHOLDERS EVER AT ODDS WITH ONE ANOTHER?

Of course stakeholders disagree. There are several reasons for the transient disagreement among levels of stakeholder (Ladson-Billings, 2016). And political influences from the outside agitate tensions even further. Education is a public good. That means everyone has a stake in the outcome, but it appears inevitable that there will be disparities among efforts to achieve that outcome (Hardin, 1968; McDonnell & Weatherford, 2016).

From large school districts to state and federal oversight of education, the institutional charge extends beyond fostering the Great Conversation. It utilizes schooling management to achieve a host of other social purposes as well. With so much included under the umbrella of schooling, a demand for accountability across the board is inevitable.

The focus in this book is limited to accountability in the educational side of schooling activities (Levin, 2012). For example, consider the evolution of the multiple-choice test item (Lindquist, 1951). A multiple-choice item is conventionally identified as *objective* because it can be machine graded. This surely sounds reasonable, does it not?

Think about it. Anything *subjective* sounds unreliable, opinionated, and deserving of suspicion and further analysis—does it not? For example, in medicine, patients are encouraged to seek one or more additional *opinions* before embarking on a course of life-threatening chemotherapy.

Subjective evaluations are slippery slopes for teachers to stand on when trying to improve their students' ability to participate in the Great Conversation. After all, how is a teacher to know whether her assessments and summary evaluations of her students' progress are on target or not?

In addition, administrators and policy-makers are hard pressed to defend institutional accountability practices if all they have is a collection of subjective opinions. In the age of quantification, the public wants data (or at least the "veil" of data, namely, numbers.) How do you show an institution is succeeding without numbers? The larger and more lumbering the system, the more important it is that numbers be sought for operational vindication.

Positive numerical change at least gives the impression that even if the truth of getting it right remains elusive, the administrators who are Level 2 stakeholders can claim that previous error has been avoided, as evidenced in demonstrable numerical improvement. Of course, as W. E. Deming and other founders of Total Quality Management always ask: "Are you sure you are relying on the right numbers?" If not, then success is not evident (Deming, 2000, 2018).

Genuine pragmatism does not seek to obfuscate with numbers. Genuine pragmatism embraces statistical and other warranting strategies if and only if they lead away from error when addressing problems and other challenges. The quest for accountability matters to pragmatists, but only to the extent that summative conclusions lead away from error in the future.

The educational scientist as a Level 3 stakeholder is much in sympathy with colleagues in the other two stakeholder levels. Like the pragmatists, they want to avoid evident error. But they want to do more. Their evidentialist approach to theory of knowledge commits them to approaching the truth of important matters as expertly as possible. In this they share much in common with the realist theories of Level 1 stakeholders.

Educational scientists investigate aggregate opinions, create tests revealing student capacities (intelligence, emotional inclinations) in some cases and student abilities in others (standardized test score assessments, knowledge of the periodic table, calculus), and they study interactive patterns among stakeholder groups and technologies. As improvements are made in data mining and neuroscience, to name two areas, new avenues for research by educational scientists continue to open up.

But caution is urged in any new science or in the rapid evolution of any new social enterprise (Taleb, 2007). What scientists learn is no sure gateway to an expected future. For example, experimental research demonstrated that most teachers tend to grade essay tests subjectively (Rosenthal & Jacobson, 1968; Rosnow & Rosenthal, 1989). Specifically, researchers found that teachers tend to give higher grades to essays that endorse a theme the teacher likes or are written by students the teacher believes are bright to begin with.

Lower grades—regardless of essay content—are given to students whom the teacher believes to be inherently less competent. In addition, other research revealed apparent racist and sexist biases (Ijalba et al., 2019). And surely religious preference and politics are subject to biased evaluations as well. Bias is destructive to appropriate evaluation and should be avoided. But bias should not be confused with the evil of prejudice. Prejudice is an intentional violation of practitioner professionalism; it is an altogether different matter.

The studies referred to above show bias, not prejudice. Humans are equipped with numerous biases by both evolution and culture. Many biases are valuable. For example, disgusting tastes and putrid smells may help people avoid toxins. Cultural norms may nudge youth away from joining gangs or using drugs. These are reasonably favored biases. But educators must discern the value of good biases from the threat of toxic biases.

Prejudice is altogether another matter. Prejudice is mean-spirited. It is much more than a simple, unintended favoring or disfavoring of one kind or another. Prejudice is often easy to spot and always to be avoided. Bias on the other hand, toxic or not, is not as easy to spot, much less track. The statistical alertness of scientists at Level 3 inform educators about bias and encourage objective approaches, minimizing the unintended consequences of compromising bias. To remove bias from the evaluation of both student progress and teacher competency, researchers favored using so-called objective items over subjective evaluation for both purposes. Their idea was that objective items are so free of bias, they can be machine graded. Problem solved?

Educational scientists are experts at creating standardized tests among many other things. Standardized tests using multiple-choice items can be efficiently graded by machine and so objectivity is achieved . . . but is it really?

Here is a test item that can be machine graded. Technically it counts as an "objective" assessment of respondent knowledge:

The best-looking person teaching this class is:

a. Rodriguez
b. Washington
c. O'Donald
d. Your instructor

Can this item be machine graded? Certainly. Does that make the item objective? In some circles still the answer would be "yes," but do you see this as an objective assessment of student knowledge? Of course not. The students may figure out the "answer" not on any grounds of knowledge, but simply because they recognize the teacher's self-obsession. But guessing another person's subjective preference is no substitute for knowledge of the world. In reality, no one but the test-maker's mother may think "d" is *truly* the answer, and even she may not be so sure!

Multiple-choice items so common in standardized testing are simply not free of subjectivity (Popham & Ryan, 2012). Certainly, they are not free of subjectivity because they can be machine graded!

Subjectivity is unavoidable in the construction of multiple-choice tests. Call this "input subjectivity" to contrast it with the "output subjectivity" of human individual evaluation of the essay tests alluded to above.

Input subjectivity shows itself in the making of tests because test-makers are unavoidably exhibiting subjectivity when choosing one subject over another for testing. Even if the choice of test content is specified not by a scientist but rather by a policy-maker, input subjectivity is in play.

Input subjectivity is also exposed in the selection of test item distractors and their wording. Volumes of expert attention continue in the never-ending search to minimize this aspect of input subjectivity (Kleinke, 2017; Woulfin & Rigby, 2017; Zhao, 2018).

Clearly, there is much to do at this most recently evolved level of stakeholder renderings of a theory of knowledge. And there are many who recognize the shortcomings and promising avenues to do better (Cuban, 2013; Darling-Hammond, 2010, 2013; Ladson-Billings, 2006; Reeves, 2011; Young, 2001).

And there is more. The phrasing of a question and the selection of distractors unavoidably reflects input subjectivity, and this has worried educational scientists for decades (Cuypers, 2004; Engel & Randall, 2009; Levin, 2012; Norris, 1989). This form of input subjectivity is so common and expected, consultants can make a living giving teacher workshops on how to prep students to answer questions they know too little about (Sugai & Tindal, 1993).

Multiple-choice tests are efficient and relatively inexpensive to use for establishing various forms of accountability, but neither efficiency nor cost are substitutes for content sensitivity or assessing students' critical breadth of reflection (Costrell et al., 2008; Rothstein et al., 2008; Siegel, 1998).

Finally, to the extent that teacher evaluations are tied to standardized test performance, the emphasis on strictly tightened rubric content tilts instruction away from teachable moments and settles on repetition of material likely to be tested (Labaree, 1997; Manley & Hawkins, 2010; Tienda, 2017). This unavoidable tilting effect is dressed up as "test alignment." In fact, it leads to "teaching to the test," and all the subjective content is embedded in the input subjectivity of test construction.

Defenders of test alignment are sticking their heads in the sand when they argue that test alignment does not prevent teachers from including other material in a class. Of course, if the teacher does teach other material, he is at risk, as are his students, of not faring well on the curriculum-restrictive test. The unspoken fact is that everyone knows, in classrooms driven by standardized multiple-choice tests, that everything that matters rests on getting "good enough" scores on those tests.

Test alignment ensures that both teachers and students are encouraged to settle for a "good enough" attitude toward instructional content (Berliner, 2006; Darling-Hammond & McLaughlin, 1995; Kohn, 2015; Koretz, 2008; Noddings, 1994; Schwartz, 1987). Strict test alignment discourages both teacher experimentation and students reaching for excellence of understanding.

This focus on test alignment, rather than the development of personal autonomy and skills at figuring things out, leaves students unprepared for unpredictable changes. These unpredictable changes are those events Nassim Taleb describes as "black swans"—outliers well off any bell-shaped distributional curve (Taleb, 2007). The term "black swan" has now become an important part of the technical literature in statistics.

Consider below a few recent facts previously commonly found in many high school STEM (science, technology, engineering, and mathematics) curricula. Technologies like Siri and Alexa are great at recalling the information they are taught. But they are not genuine students. They are machines. Genuine students need to learn how to evaluate and manage facts and not simply recognize alleged facts in response to systematic prompts.

Mineralogists once had a hardness standard from 1 to 10. It was considered a fact that all hardness could be measured and calibrated on this taxonomy because one could observe which minerals were able to scratch others. According to the apparent exactness of the relevant science, there was no substance harder than diamonds, which were rated 10. Manufactured diamonds were the real thing if they could match the hardness standards. Then it happened—a black swan!

Some enterprising Japanese scientists created hyperdiamonds. Hyperdiamonds are beyond the standard scale for measuring hardness (James, 2019). These artificial diamonds are harder than natural diamonds, and thus harder than anything in the previously known world. And this spectacular event happened just a few years ago!

An alleged fact of astrophysics a few years ago was that nothing falling into a black hole ever escaped, but then Stephen Hawking and Roger Penrose made the case for black hole radiation—thus an "escape" (Penrose, 2005). A gene exposing heavy smokers to even greater risk of lung cancer was discovered in the early twenty-first century (Pearl & MacKenzie, 2018).

The point is that coming across the unexpected is part and parcel of participating in the Great Conversation (Gigerenzer, 2008). Curricula that sacrifice creation of a community of inquiry in favor of test preparation cannot prepare students for participation in the Great Conversation. Curricula that focus on test alignment are not preparing students for black swans, large and small, that occur in everyone's life from time to time. Achievement in thinking skill is different from excellence in recognition of likely multiple-choice answers (Baron, 2007; Newell et al., 1958; Scheffler, 1973).

Educational scientists are aware of these challenges. The continued existence of certain testing practices does not mean these challenges are being ignored. It simply is a fact of life in education, medicine, and many technological fields that the range and depth of challenges exceeds scientists' understanding. Progress is being made by Level 3 stakeholders and will continue, but they must continually engage stakeholders' insights from the other two levels.

The fact that each level of stakeholder begins with a different theory of knowledge is not an impediment to progress. The three different approaches to theory of knowledge may inform, balance, and fuel a productive advance the changing world ahead. As it stands, it should already be evident that all levels recognize that education, as opposed to mere schooling, should advance each student's reach for excellence of achievement—always! This shared purpose cannot be realized in a schooling system driven by standardized measurements and rubrics focused on detecting proportionate levels of "good enough."

Level 3 stakeholders have illuminated much about what is happening in large-scale schooling management and accountability (Arrow et al., 2000). They also have drawn attention to gaps existing in the development of student critical thinking, autonomy, and virtues of relentless truth-seeking (Stich & Nisbett, 1980). Each of these so crucial to the vision articulated by Level 1 stakeholders (Norris, 1995). And each is included in the ambitions of Level 2 stakeholders (Tishman & Perkins, 1993). But there is so much more to do.

Successful collaboration among stakeholders must begin with a renewed focus by all on the concept of *student*. What is a student? Is a student simply an animated part in a schooling system or a convenient product of socialization appealing to those in power? What makes a learner genuinely a student? What makes a student better? How can students be both schooled and educated successfully?

STUDENT-CENTERED, TRUTH-VALUING AMBITIONS

Christopher Winch, Matthew Lipman, Alison Gopnik, Alfie Kohn, and Theodore Gormley are just a few of the theorists and researchers who focus renewed attention to the vision of a Level 1 stakeholder theory of knowledge, values, and virtues (Winch, 2006; Lipman, 2003; Gopnik, 2009, 2016; Gopnik et al., 1999; Kohn, 2015; Gormley, 2017). Here we encounter the scaffolding for student building that is already millennia old (Mlodinow, 2015; Tattersall & Desalle, 2019; Tomasello, 2014, 2019).

To realize the vision of student building, changes in the schooling system need to be made. Changes in classroom instruction need to be made. Bringing stakeholder levels into alignment with the theories of knowledge that naturally animate each level, must acknowledge the commitments of the other levels and then work together to develop dynamically shared ambitions without loss of identity to any stakeholder level. Now, how to do this?

Proper alignment must begin with shared understanding of the meaning of student. The concept *student* cuts across generations and geographic lines (Mercier & Sperber, 2017; Mlodinow, 2015, 2018). Roughly speaking, students are *those purposefully learning to engage the physical, social, and cultural worlds they encounter. Purposefully* makes the learning other than chance or mere socialization. Students want to know how and why things are as they are. Students anticipate having a role in the life ahead.

Obviously, the concept of student prompts reflection on the concept of learning and, even more so, on the value of learning. Across generations, across cultural and geographic divides, a minimal consensus of learning is uncontroversial. Learning is bringing to mind information. Most animals learn. The information they seek is for specific purposes of the moment, whereas human learners often seek abstractions and counterfactuals beyond the immediate (Tattersall & Desalle, 2019).

Further details about learning can be set aside for now. Whether learning is experiential, culturally derived, hardwired, developmentally responsive, and so on, all of these factors are entailed by the general definition above of what, roughly speaking, learning is. *What* is to be learned (Level 1 and Level 2), and *when* (Level 2 and Level 3), and *how* (Level 2 and Level 3) are some of the details left for a later time.

A focus on the general concept of *student* prompts reflection on motivation. Motivation is animated change from a state of mental inertia. Animated change is not directionless. Numerous developmental psychologists have experimentally demonstrated that children are learning from their environment shortly after they are born, and this is prior to any enculturation forces have any influence (Bloom, 2005; Gopnik, 2009; Gopnik et al., 1999).

By two to three years old, the problem-solving skills of human children are already a match for all other adult primate cousins (Tomasello, 2019). This amplification of student building forces is largely the result of enculturation with episodes of deliberate teaching and the richly textured languages humans have developed (Tomasello, 2019; Wiley, 2015).

In addition, another student-building trait humans acquire is demonstrable capacity for evaluating arguments and other abstractions, a capacity well beyond that of any other animals. Participation in community leads from evolving capacities to tangible abilities (Sapolsky, 2018).

In short, schooling, education, and general absorption in local culture all contribute to the development of reasoning humans. The concept of local culture is dynamic in its influence inasmuch as local cultures immersed in electronic media are much more multipotent than cultures that are more parochial because of geographic, political, or other limitations.

The attributes and influences of student building mentioned above contribute to the continued development of the physiology of the brain's frontal lobes until a student's early 20s (Sapolsky, 2018). If successful, student building leads to autonomous dispositions towards abstraction, evaluation, and critical-creative thinking for the rest of an individual's life.

Learning that becomes more focused on general evaluations and imaginative abstractions is key to moving humans from mere learners to students (Mercier & Sperber, 2017). It is this intentionality to understand the world and not just local problems that makes human beings students and not mere learners (Mercier & Sperber, 2017; Tomasello, 2014; 2019). *Students participate in the Great Conversation as no mere learner can or is even inclined to.*

GETTING IT APPROXIMATELY RIGHT WHILE KNOWING SOME OF IT WILL BE WRONG

Not one of the stakeholder levels eschews the idea of truth. All could presumably agree on Alfred Tarski's (1944) characterization of the concept of truth which states that a representation X is true if and only if reality is X. But this presumed agreement does not extend to a metaphysical account of truth. Nor does the agreement extend to the details of a semantic or other representational account of truth. The idea of truth here is at best simply reality itself or a heuristic at worst.

As a heuristic notion, truth can be identified as that which anchors each theory of knowledge across the three levels. In this role of anchoring knowledge, the concept of truth keeps knowledge claims from degenerating into freewheeling opinion or an object deserving the intellectual scorn of skeptics.

Truth as referring to representation of reality simpliciter gives a more robust foundation for the aims of any productive theory of knowledge (Williamson, 2000; Blackburn, 2018). In the spirit of Thomas Kuhn we can say, "I am a physicist! Of course, I think there is a reality out there about which we can be right or wrong." However, truth and knowledge should not be confused. Truth is what knowledge is *about*. Knowledge and truth are not the same thing.

Saying there is a truth to the question about how many fingers I have extended may be aligned with observing and counting my extended fingers, but alignment and identity are not one and the same, even when the alignment is wholly free of variance at every level of possible analysis. The theories of knowledge foundational to educational practice converge on this general concept of truth, despite having grounds for dispute between conflicting theories of knowledge.

In an important sense, each theory of knowledge is a truth-seeking guide for the levels of educational stakeholders. What all stakeholders share is a commitment to truth-seeking even if, as pragmatists might claim, the ostensible goal is merely the avoidance of error. Truth-seeking invigorates the Great Conversation. Truth-seeking invigorates the search for utility in schooling operations. And truth-seeking demands strict attention to warranting among evidentialists.

Realists seek knowledge in matters large and small that map onto the world as the world in fact is. An empty gas tank is an empty gas tank. Truth and knowledge *may be* in perfect alignment in such cases. In contrast, many educators believe we need to learn the truth about how to motivate students to become learners. Such a truth is very deep and perhaps inaccessible to error-free human knowing. Yet is that not a truth worth pursuing as a central to educational success?

Evolutionary psychologists are likely to suggest that searching for the truth of more accurate ways to motivate students is blinding educators to the real challenge of motivational truth. Evolutionary psychologists have increasingly found that, like other mammals, human infants are brought into the world with an inherent tendency to learn. Indeed, the truth that educators should seek is: "What are we doing to drive the motivation to learn out of students?"

A realist response to this challenge is to take it seriously. In their never-ending search for truth, realists should never become absolutists. In fact, realists ought to always be the first ones to take intellectual challenges seriously because they are committed to aligning knowledge claims with actual reality. To the realist, a challenge to a knowledge claim involving a deep truth such as human motivation ought to be taken seriously *always* (Littlejohn, 2012).

In short, realists appreciate that the goal of alignment is not the same as demanding that truth and knowledge be treated as identical accomplishments. Knowledge aligning with truth is an achievement (Bradford, 2015). Some of those achievements, such as about an empty gas tank, are shallow and of less general consequence than deeper questions about such things as human nature, particle physics, mathematical group theory, and so on. But in all cases realists want knowledge to align with reality as much as possible (Moore, 1959).

The deeper the question, the more notable any alignment between truth and knowledge becomes. The more closely aligned knowledge becomes to truth, the more it should be valued as an accomplishment (Bradford, 2015). And, the deeper the question, the more tolerance there must be for the possibility that current knowledge claims may be in error.

Pragmatists want to avoid error. This means that pragmatists want to distance themselves from conclusions and practices that get things wrong. Level 2 stakeholders represent policy-makers and administrators typically. These stakeholders are expected to ensure accountability in how school systems operate. Budgets must be balanced, food services must be safe, the buses must run on time, litigation should be minimized, politicians appeased, and opportunities for student-building participation in the Great Conversation of Humankind must be managed.

Since the 1990s there has been a push to use inexpensive and efficient standardized tests to determine state, district, school, and classroom accountability. The operative questions are: "Which tests are the best?" "What processes are affordable?" "What processes effectively distinguish between success and failure in both schooling and educational operations?" In responding to these questions, mere opinion, even professional opinion, is insufficient for avoiding error in evaluating institutional effectiveness in education.

The most conspicuous challenge to which all seem to agree is that student learning should be evaluated. The educational sciences have learned much about learning. Seemingly, numerous resources are readily available for measuring student learning. All that remains to be done is scaling measurement operations and standardizing aggregations of performance. Is this error minimizing solution adequately meeting the challenges of education accountability?

In a word: no. Learning is certainly relevant to student building, but it does not comport well with all the hopes and ambitions stakeholders share in bringing students to a life of participation in the Great Conversation. Measuring recognition learning is relatively cheap and efficient, but it is ineffective as a reasonably comprehensive summary of schooling success in matters of education.

In addition, policy-makers have increasingly come to recognize that the burden placed on administrators and their subordinates has led to further error rather than moving away from error in educational evaluation. Not only are teachers teaching to the test, but school districts are holding workshops and hiring "experts" to help folks scam test items when they did not recognize an answer. And there was more: cheating among educators was a growing concern.

Social psychology and anthropological studies have made it unquestionably clear that so much of learning is enculturation. And role-modeling is the major facet of enculturation (Posner, 1986; Sturt et al., 2004; Tomasello, 2014). When teachers and administrators become cheats—especially in their professional behavior—the enculturation effect on students is frightening to even imagine.

The extent of cheating and manipulating the schooling system is noted in chapter 4. Strategies for circumventing the intent and purpose of accountability systems are proliferating (Cohen et al., 2017; Kane & Staiger, 2002). Outright cheating is ubiquitous (Magee, 2016; Pell, 2012; Rolland, 2012; Strauss, 2016; Woodall, 2015).

Pragmatic stakeholders must see that schooling accountability systems have gone awry (Kraft & Gilmour, 2017). Error in system management is increasing rather than decreasing over the past several decades (Harris & Harrington, 2006; Reback et al., 2017). Any theory of knowledge that accommodates increasing rates of error is far from the spirit of pragmatism (Mendell, 1995).

Level 2 stakeholders committed to a pragmatic theory of knowledge have little choice but to abort current practices that critics such as Berliner (Level 3), Ravitch (Level 3), and Koretz (himself a Level 2 policy-maker) lament, and search for a less objectionable way to work with all stakeholders in education.

Level 3 stakeholders seem in some ways to be nearly paralyzed by the current situation. It was the educational scientists who produced measures of learning that were utilized by Level 2 stakeholders to improve education from top to bottom. It has also been the work of many educational scientists that shows much that should be evaluated is not evaluated, given current protocols and measurement apparatus (Darling-Hammond & McLaughlin, 1995; Menken, 2006; Norris, 1995). What to do?

A step forward is to acknowledge that successful measurement of learning, which scientists are very good at, is not the same as measuring the success of student building. Reliable recognition of responses to test items does not lead to further respect for fellow learners, evaluation of shared hypotheses, passion for truth-seeking, or collaborative participation in the Great Conversation of Humankind.

The consequences of this oversight are that research into the educational development of students is overshadowed by a focus on learning measurement systems that lend themselves to relatively inexpensive and efficient accountability systems producing data that Level 2 stakeholders hold out to nonprofessionals as quantitative evidence of some kind of success. The nature of the alleged success is opaque in terms of traditional education ambitions.

Learning measurements, even in the absence of cheating or other attempts to manipulate the data, testify solely to minimal information acquisition on the part of learners that is useful in recognizing a likely answer out of a set of alternatives. But is that really so important?

Siri, Alexa, and other search engines already know so much more information than any human ever will. In addition, most students have ready access to that data. Learning measurements accurately testify to the success of loading data recognition to learners over the short run. But all educational professionals need to ask: "Is that so important?"

Educational scientists need to further studies into the entire process of student building. The educational sciences must become more broadly robust in scope. Level 2 stakeholders must be patient and not grasp at straws for remediating a failing system, but instead must focus on social architectures in the classroom that will allow teachers to host and invite students into the Great Conversation of Humankind (Wagner et al., 2016, 2017, 2018).

All invested in education should recognize that, given educational scientists' time and money for research, recommendations for improved classroom and schooling practices for student building will emerge. But none of this will happen because of threats or cries of urgency. As the founder of the TQM movement, W. Edwards Deming, warned, for systems to work leaders must first and foremost drive out fear (Deming, 2000).

In addition, as the TQM advocates recognized, accountability should focus only on a few numbers and review their relevancy periodically (Deming, 2000, 2018; Defeo, 2014). Simply data mining and accumulating massive amounts of data serves only to keep stakeholders from seeing the forest for the trees.

Much has been learned about student building, and there is much more to learn. Simple learning strategies, whether derived from animal experimentation, machine learning, or human recognition studies, will not reveal what stakeholders need to understand about student building. Instead, progress is made through the commitment of researchers to an evidentialist theory of knowledge. Knowledge advances not smoothly, but in jerks and spurts. To count as knowledge, remember that the evidentialists demand that conclusions be tied to credible warrants.

If you ever had an educational statistics class and it was taught like a bad class in culinary arts where you did nothing more than accumulate a list of recipes—beware! That is outside the responsible realm of any professional stakeholder group in education. Statistics are to be learned in order to evaluate knowledge claims and show tools of warrant for advancing claims of one's own.

Matters are even worse if a subsequent research methodology class was similarly taught as learning a catalog of recipes. In truth, research methodology classes are philosophy classes. Research methodology is a theory of knowledge class set within a discipline. It is meant to raise vital questions and offer proposals answering the question: How does one know that X is likely true? Current standards of warranting and justification are reviewed and evaluated in principle.

The advanced student in research methodology needs first and foremost to recognize that questions of research methodology are far from settled (Page, 2001). Limits on the value of tests of significance as sample sizes grow large, regression to the mean as a limitation on social or genetic inheritance, path analysis, Bayesianism versus descriptive statistics, and many more topics are revisited from time to time as methodologists reconstruct systems they conclude are of proper warrant (Freedman, 2009; Merton, 1973; Simon, 1954; Stigler, 2016).

Cries of urgency are distracting to both relevant research and programmatic implementation. Getting more things right than not, is good. Surely all can agree on that (Williamson, 2005). Reducing error in research and policy programmatic protocols are all good things. And again, in principle it should be obvious that all stakeholders can agree to the value of reduced error in research, programmatic development, and classroom practice. But such good things and their values cannot be purchased on demand. Creating a sense of urgency is more likely to hinder productive advance than to prompt it.

Forcing urgency in research, policy-making, or programmatic protocols often does no more than paralyze an otherwise productive and evolving system. This is true in education as much as it is in, say, medicine. Truth is not available on demand to anyone at any time. It must be earned and shown to be warrantable (Conee & Feldman, 2004; DeRose, 2000; Fantl & McGrath, 2009). Educators would do all stakeholders more good by borrowing from medicine the caveat: FIRST, DO NO HARM.

STAYING ON THE SAME PAGE

So educational stakeholders agree across the board that it is important, firstly, that no stakeholder or stakeholder group should do harm. Second, it should be abundantly clear by now that educators as a group cannot fulfill their ambitions by advocating skepticism or eschewing the search for truth in any way. Truth-seeking, even for pragmatists intent on avoidance of error, is an ambition shared properly by all stakeholders in education. And there is more.

Educators alert to advances in anthropology, evolutionary psychology, and the other social sciences in general must surely accept that there is substantial difference between the development of recognition learning processes and the development of student building. Recognition learning is common in the evolution of most mammals, humans included. But humans alone became student builders (Pasnau, 2017; Scheffler, 2009). Students have skills, attitudes, and values in addition to learning (Mlodinow, 2015; Sapolsky, 2018; Tattersall & DeSalle, 2019; Tomasello, 2014, 2019). As with the first two across-the-board agreements, this third focus on student building should similarly bring all educational stakeholder levels together in common ambition.

As a fourth focus, all levels of stakeholder will better serve themselves and all others involved in education by recognizing that their shared ambitions bring them together in a noble cause, namely, creating and sustaining the Great Conversation of Humankind (Wagner et al., 2018).

Finally, the three levels of stakeholders need to be alert to the differences in a theory of knowledge animating each level's practices. Tolerance for these distinctions is indispensable for staying on the same page. Theory of knowledge distinctions need not lead to the disparagement of another level's expert concerns. The distinctions among the three levels in education may actually fuel both truth-seeking and student building.

A REASONABLE HOPE

There is reason for hope. Taking the simplest and perhaps most memorable route, please consider a robust understanding of a law alluded to previously, namely, the Law of Figuring Things Out. This guiding principle transcends, that is to say, accommodates all three theories of stakeholder knowledge commitments. A robust understanding of the Law of Figuring Things Out brings together all of the common concerns that were reviewed in the previous section.

The Law of Figuring Things Out is not a theory of knowledge. It is a cognitive process fueled by learning instincts, by problem-framing skills, by the use of acquired inferential warranting practices, and by a passion for advancing current understanding bit by bit.

The Law of Figuring Things Out begins with a general concern (Wagner et al., 2018). Subsequently, this general concern is followed by framing an appropriate problem space (Tversky & Kahneman, 1981). A theory of knowledge must be employed implicitly at least to narrow the focus from a mere general concern to an explicit problem space. A theory of knowledge will then sanction intellectual moves that license plausible conclusions or warrant grounds for drawing inferences and proposing subsequent action.

That is pretty much it. The Law of Figuring Things Out defines well the cognitive structure of the Great Conversation. However, the Great Conversation must also be augmented by many psychological and moral commitments and strategies as well (Peters, 1966; Siegel, 1999, 2017). Respect for other participants, passion for truth-seeking, and zeal for problem solving are as central to the Great Conversation as is the necessary cognitive structures.

Barbara Tversky is surely the dean of educational psychology today. She is also one of a handful of the world's great empirical researchers in the science of psychology generally. Her hundreds of research articles and several books could be cited as supporting the cognitive processes grounding the Law of Figuring Things Out. The reader is directed to her recent book, *Mind in Motion* (Tversky 2019).

Tversky's work does not address all of the Law, or the associated concepts central to this book of student building and the Great Conversation, but her empirical studies establish the claims that the Law is not a theory of knowledge but rather a process that accommodates each of the stakeholder theories and the passion for truth-seeking that unifies the levels of stakeholder practice.

Educational stakeholders are not only responsible for hosting the Great Conversation, but stakeholder collaboration among levels requires all to recognize that applying the Law of Figuring Things Out in this case is itself an instance of the Great Conversation and requires that all the relevant psychological and moral commitments be in place as well. The separate theories of knowledge relied upon by the respective stakeholder levels does not prohibit shared truth-seeking about how to best educate and build students.

You have no doubt heard the phrase, "No man is an island." So it is with the stakeholder levels and their respective theories of knowledge. No one of the three stakeholder levels has the resources within itself to carry out such an enormous task. The Law of Figuring Things Out requires that all resources be put on the table in order to make it possible for our attempts to get things done to be successful.

SUMMARY, RECOMMENDATIONS, AND CAVEATS

Summary

1. The world changes, so what is knowable changes as well. This realization should fuel truth-seeking rather than discourage it.
2. Education is of central importance, but truth-seeking by professionals to optimize secure schooling practices, policies, and protocols is essential to stakeholders as well.
3. Student building, as described here, is key to bringing students into lifetime engagement with the Great Conversation.
4. Achievement in thinking skills is different from adequacy in recognition skills for selecting likely multiple-choice responses on standardized tests. Student building aims at the first skill. Competency in the second skill is perhaps best illustrated in the downloading process for enhancing machine recollection intelligence as relied on by Apple's Siri, Google, and other search engines.
5. Successful cooperation and collaboration among stakeholders relies on three central concepts that transcend but can be superimposed on any of theories of knowledge discussed, namely student building, the Great Conversation, and the Law of Figuring Things Out.

Recommendations

1. Continuous improvement in organizational policy and practice relies on important quantified data. But be sure to review data assessment practices to ensure that the right numbers are the focus. An array of big data must not detract from meaningful evaluation. Only meaningful data evaluation can effectively serve continuous improvement in planning (Deming, 2018).

2. Truth-seeking on the part of educational professionals should aim at developing truth-seeking as part of student building at every level of schooling.
3. Never confuse bias and prejudice. Some biases are valuable and should not be discouraged. On the other hand, prejudice is nothing but mean-spirited bias and should always be discouraged.
4. When the work of educational professionals is tied to strictly confining, rubric-defined content, instruction tilts away from taking advantage of teachable moments to repetition of material likely to be assessed in standardized multiple-choice fashion (Wagner et al., 2018).
5. Focus on test alignment often endangers developing capable and autonomous thinking. Capable autonomous thinking is necessary for the vagaries of engagement with real-life "black swan" challenges (Taleb, 2007).
6. Student building is inherently moral. It aims at developing respect for truth and for others. It aims for excellence of performance and eschews "good enough" thinking.

Caveats

1. Be careful not to limit knowledge claims merely to those which seem to rely solely on empirical support. Empirical support always rests on a platform of assumptions and reason. Knowledge claims also benefit from metaphor, analogy, and artistic depictions which can be truth revealing (Elgin, 2017; Goodman & Elgin, 1988; Wright, 1921).
2. Remember, no observations, no matter how carefully managed, are theory free (Hanson, 1958).
3. "Black Swans," those events that are so far off the Gaussian curve that they can never be reasonably anticipated, are sure to happen. Maintain a sense of mental agility in truth-seeking practices to adapt to accommodating outlier effects (Taleb, 2007).
4. Measuring educational success using only standardized multiple-choice tests is a halfhearted effort at managing programmatic progress. Look for more robust evaluational identifiers to complement the inexpensive and simple monitoring standardized testing offers.
5. Subjectivity, either "input subjectivity" or "output subjectivity," should be acknowledged and its effects minimized as much as possible.

6. In practice, "test alignment" often erodes into "teaching to the test" (Kohn, 2015; Koretz, 2017; Wagner et al., 2018).

Glossary

autonomy: The capacity to override wants and desires.

bivariate distribution: A probability distribution that for each of two variables (X and Y) will fall into a discrete range of values. (This generalizes to multiple variables which is termed a multivariate distribution.)

Brownian motion: Robert Brown was a Scottish botanist who noticed random fluctuations of pollen particles in a fluid. Since then the term Brownian motion is often used to denote random fluctuation of particles in any medium. Einstein used the term in creating the probabilistic architecture of early quantum theory.

commitment: Sustained and willful dedication to a cause.

confounder: Refers to influences that disrupt an otherwise obvious causal path and thereby mislead investigators.

contextualism: Often seen as a variant of contemporary pragmatism. For contextualists, the proper framing of an investigation determines the most apt judgment to follow. Framing the problem space is the most important step in advancing knowledge.

correlation coefficient: A numerical measure of a statistical relationship between two variables in a given data set.

correspondence theory: The realist belief that judgments about how the world is are true only to the extent that those judgments map onto the world exactly and without error—evident or not.

counterfactual reflection: Refers to imagining what might have happened had things been different in some way.

covariance: The extent to which change in one variable can be seen producing an effect in another variable.

default position: A general practice for problem-solving utilized when there is no apparent strategy for securing certainty of judgment.

didactic instruction: Information delivered in a strictly organized way by an expert usually following a precisely defined rubric. Does not encourage Socratic dialogue or shared evaluation of the material's intellectual merit.

dispositions: Inclinations to behave in predictable ways in the presence of relevant cues. These inclinations are not to be confused with skills or attitudes of any sort.

doxastic attitudes: The various mental stances that one can take with regard to a proposed belief, like confidently believing it, disbelieving it, or withholding judgment either way.

education: To distinguish education from the concept of *schooling,* education in this book refers to the virtues, skills, and dispositions consistent with the idea of building student readiness for participation in the Great Conversation of Humankind.

epistemic/epistemology: From the ancient Greek *episteme*, these terms refer to theorizing about the meaning of the concept of *knowledge.* Note here the focus on the term knowledge.

existential angst: An identity crisis wherein one feels separate and apart from what appears to be a discomforting and alien surround.

foundationalism: A theory of knowledge that asserts there must be a single standard of knowledge that all knowledge claims must reflect.

Gaussian curve: Named after the great mathematician Carl Gauss, this is also known as the "bell-shaped curve." Many natural characteristics such as height, weight, life spans, and intelligence of various species tends to center around a mean and taper off to fewer examples of differentiation to the left and right of the mean.

Hegelian system-building: Hegel was a nineteenth century philosopher who tried summing up the architecture of all that exists both naturally and beyond through a grand schema. Today when people offer overly grand schemes to explain everything, they might be accused of Hegelian system-building.

instrumentalism: The view that our ideas are merely instruments valuable to the extent they allow us to predict outcomes and cope with the world.

Claims ideas should not be thought of as representations of an underlying reality.

internal realist/external realist: All realists believe there is a world about which judgments can be made that are either correct or incorrect. For internal realists such as Hilary Putnam, those judgments must fit the conceptual apparatus of thinkers. For external realists such as Alfred Tarski, those judgments must align with the world external to mind.

intersubjective agreement: When subjective bias cannot be eliminated or managed, people can still achieve some overlapping agreement of observations and commitments.

isomorphism: When members of two sets of things can be ordered and aligned perfectly, they are said to be related in isomorphic fashion. The idea originated in mathematics wherein technical alignment is pristine and evident.

knowing that/ knowing how: knowing *that* something is true, such as "George Washington is president," is a different sort of knowing than knowing *how* to encourage a student to persist in her studies.

Law of Figuring Things Out: adaptationist strategies to frame and make sense of challenges. This does not always lead to well-defined solutions and may depend on intuitions, analogies, and metaphorical, and counterfactual imagination, all in order to get beyond a currently imposed shared understanding of a community.

linear correlation: The degree to which a pair of variables are linearly related. This is to say that given the data at hand, a change in one variable seems to be accompanied by change in another well-defined, independent variable.

mentalist/objectivist: Refers to the determining source of an observer/ thinker's doxastic attitude. A mentalistic attitude or belief is a result of mental architecture and prior beliefs. In contrast, an objectivist attitude or belief is one prompted by impressions made by the world external to the mind.

metaphysics: Any theory about the fundamental constituents of reality.

moral nihilism: In contrast to forms of moral relativism that may license the rightness of each person's position given his or her psychological make-up, this denies any meaningfulness to moral reflection or prescription.

nihilism: A position of extreme skepticism concluding that nothing can be understood as an instance of reality.

null hypothesis: The hypothesis that there is no significant difference between sample groups under study. Any difference is due to sampling error. Such errors are presumably detected by (p-values) tests of significance.

objectively: Perceptions and judgments made without bias.

operational definition: Defines terms in virtue of operations. For example, a stick of arbitrary length is defined as a "foot." Six feet would be determined by laying the stick end to end five times from the original position. Thus, IQ can be defined as whatever score a person gets on a standardized IQ test. Consequently, in this view IQ is not defined by some suspicious metaphysical, nonobservable notion of intelligence.

path analysis: A mathematical model to interpret correlation in complex causal systems using non-experimental data. The paths are identified by asking, "Would X have occurred but for the occurrence of Y?"

plausible: A reasonable position to take in light of the evidence available at the moment.

reliabilism: Acknowledges the reality of truth but believes access to it impossible. Reliabilism instead encourages knowledge seekers to determine the dependability of a process for knowing and advises them to stick with that process without further efforts to warrant the legitimacy of the process.

schooling: The logistical and management plans, practices, and protocols that are intended to secure operational efficiency for socialization and, ultimately, the education of students.

skeptic: An extreme skeptic is someone who denies all possibility of knowledge or ever approaching truth.

skills: Capacities transformed into abilities and put into service by those who have acquired the abilities.

social constructionism: A theory of knowledge that is based not on evidence of reality, but rather on what ideas a community of people agree on at a given time.

standard deviation: Indicates how far awry an individual observation is from the center of a Gaussian (bell-shaped) distribution curve.

transducer-caused disparity: Disparity arising when impressions made on the mind by observing the world do not align well with how the world in fact is.

validity: Rather than a synonym for the word truth, validity or, more specifically, the concept of deductive validity, refers to the form of an argument in which, assuming the truth of the premises and the rules of formal logic, the conclusion is guaranteed to be true. A simplified example from hypothesis testing would be (1) *if* the hypothesis is true, *then* this is the predicted result we should be able to observe, but (2) we did *not* get that result, so therefore (3) the hypothesis is false. This form is known as "denying the consequent" because the statement in premise (2) denies the consequent of premise (1) and that generates the conclusion in (3).

variables: A defined feature or object that is liable to forces of change.

virtues: Commitments and accompanying dispositions to act and speak in ways that contribute to personal or collective well-being.

References

Achinstein, P. (2019). *Speculation within and about science*. New York, NY: Oxford University Press.

Agasisti, T., & Zoido, P. (2018). Comparing the efficiency of schools through international benchmarking: Results from an empirical analysis of OECD PISA 2012 data. *Educational Researcher, 47*(6), 352–362.

Aikin, S. (2014). *Evidentialism and the will to believe*. New York, NY: Bloomsbury Publishing.

American Statistical Association. (2014, April). ASA Statement on using value-added models for educational assessment. https://www.amstat.org/asa/files/pdfs/POL-ASAVAM-Statement.pdf

Amrein-Beardsley, A., & Collins, C. (2012). The SAS education value-added assessment system (SAS® EVAAS®) in the Houston Independent School District (HISD): Intended and unintended consequences. *Education Policy Analysis Archives, 20*(12), 1–28. epaa.asu.edu/ojs/article/ view/1096

Arrow, K., Bowles, S., & Durlauf, S. (Eds.). (2000). *Meritocracy and economic inequality*. Princeton, NJ: Princeton University Press.

Auerbach, D. (2018). *Bitwise*. New York, NY: Pantheon.

Ayer, A. J. (1968). *The origins of pragmatism*. New York, NY: Macmillan.

Bailin, S., & Battersby, M. (2017). What should I believe? *Teaching Philosophy, 40*(3), 275–295.

Baker, L. (2007). *The metaphysics of everyday life*. New York, NY: Cambridge University Press.

Bandura, A. (1976). *Social learning theory*. Upper Saddle River, NJ: Prentice-Hall.

Banks, J. (1998). The lives and values of researchers: Implications for educating citizens in a multicultural society. *Educational Researcher, 27*(5), 4–17.

Bareinboim, E., & Pearl, J. (2012). Causal inference by surrogate experiments: z-identifiability. In N. de Freitas & K. Murphy (Eds.), *Proceedings of the Twenty-Eighth Conference on Uncertainty in Artificial Intelligence* (pp. 113–120). Corvallis, OR: AUAI Press.

Baron, J. (2007). *Thinking and deciding* (4th ed.). New York, NY: Cambridge University Press.

Baron, J., & Hershey, J. (1988). Outcome bias in decision evaluation. *Journal of Personality and Social Psychology, 54*(4), 569–579.

Becker, A. (2018). *What is real?: The unfinished quest for the meaning of quantum physics.* New York, NY: Basic Books.

Berger, P., & Luckmann, T. (1966). *The social construction of reality.* New York, NY: Anchor Books.

Berliner, D. C. (2006). Our impoverished view of educational reform. *Teachers College Record, 108*(6), 949–995.

Berliner, D. C., & Biddle, B. J. (1995). *The manufactured crisis: Myths, fraud, and the attack on America's public schools.* New York, NY: Basic Books

Berliner, D. & Glass, G. (2014). *Fifty myths and lies that threaten America's public schools: The real crisis in education.* New York, NY: Teachers College Press.

Beth, E., & Piaget, J. (1974). *Mathematical epistemology and psychology.* Dordrecht, The Netherlands: D. Reidel.

Blackburn, S. (2005). *Truth: A guide.* New York, NY: Oxford University Press.

Blackburn, S. (2018). *On truth.* New York, NY: Oxford University Press.

Blaylock, H. (1964). *Causal inference in nonexperimental research.* Chapel Hill, NC: University of North Carolina Press.

Blinder, A. (2015, April 2). Atlanta educators convicted in school cheating scandal. *New York Times.* https://www.nytimes.com/2015/04/02/us/verdict-reached-in-atlanta-school-testing-trial.html

Bloom, P. (2005). *Descartes' baby: How the science of child development explains what makes us human.* New York, NY: Basic Books.

Bloom, P. (2016). *Against empathy: The case for rational compassion.* New York, NY: Ecco.

Booher-Jennings, J. (2005). Below the bubble: Educational triage and the Texas accountability system. *American Educational Research Journal, 42*(2), 231–268.

Box, J. F. (1978). *R. A. Fisher: The life of a scientist.* New York, NY: John Wiley.

Bradford, G. (2015). *Achievement.* New York, NY: Oxford University Press.

Brighouse, H., Ladd, H. F., Loeb, S., & Swift, A. (2018). *Educational goods: Values, evidence, and decision-making.* Chicago, IL: University of Chicago Press.

Brown, E. (2013, April 12). Teachers in 18 D.C. classrooms cheated on tests last year, probe finds. *Washington Post.* https://www.washingtonpost.com/local/education/teachers-in-18-dc-classrooms-cheated-on-tests-last-year-probe-finds/2013/04/12/b1a57e7c-a3a3-11e2-82bc-511538ae90a4_story.html

Burge, T. (2010). *Origins of objectivity.* New York, NY: Oxford University Press.

Burks, B. S. (1926). On the inadequacy of the partial and multiple correlation technique: parts 1 and 2. *Journal of Experimental Psychology, 17*(8), Part 1, 532–540; Part 2, 625–630.

Campbell, D. T. (1975). Assessing the impact of planned social change. In G. M Lyons (Ed.), *Social Research and Public Policies: The Dartmouth/OECD Conference.* Hanover, NH: Dartmouth College. http://citeseerx.ist.psu.edu/viewdoc/download?doi=10.1.1.170.6988&rep=rep1&type=pdf

Campbell-Whatley, G., Hancock, D., & Dunaway, D. (2016). *A school leader's guide to implementing the Common Core.* New York, NY: CRC Press.

Caplan, B. (2018). *The case against education: Why the system is a waste of time and money.* Princeton, NJ: Princeton University Press.

Carey, N. (2015). *Junk DNA.* New York, NY: Columbia University Press.

Carnoy, M., & Loeb, S. (2003). Does external accountability affect student outcomes? A cross-state analysis. *Educational Evaluation and Policy Analysis, 24*(4), 305–331.

Cheng, E. (2018). *The art of logic in an illogical world.* New York, NY: Basic Books.

Chisholm, R. (1982). *The foundations of knowing.* Minneapolis, MN: University of Minnesota Press.

Chomsky, N. (1959). A review of B. F. Skinner's *Verbal Behavior*. *Language*, *35*(1), 26–58.

Church, A. (1936). An unsolvable problem of elementary number theory. *American Journal of Mathematics 58*(2): 345–363. doi:10.2307/2371045

Coburn, C., Heather, C. & Spillane, J. (2016). Alignment and accountability in policy design and implementation: The Common Core State Standards and implementation research. *Educational Researcher*, *45*(4), 243–251.

Coburn, C., & Stein, M. (Eds.). (2010). *Research and practice in education: Building alliances, bridging the divide*. Lanham, MD: Rowman & Littlefield.

Cohen, D., Spillane, J., & Peurach, D. (2017). The dilemmas of educational reform. *Educational Researcher*, *47*(3), 204–212.

Cole, S., & Herman, M. (2002). Fallibility in estimating direct effects. *International Journal of Epidemiology*, *31*(1), 163–165.

Coles, G. (2003). *Reading the naked truth: Literacy, legislation, and lies*. Portsmouth, NH: Heinemann.

Conee, E., & Feldman, R. (2004). *Evidentialism*. New York, NY: Clarendon Press.

Conee, E., & Feldman, R. (2011). Reply to Duncan Pritchard. In T. Dougherty (Ed.), *Evidentialism and its discontents* (pp. 289–292). New York, NY: Oxford University Press.

Costrell, R., Hanushek, E., & Loeb, S. (2008). What do cost functions tell us about the cost of an adequate education? *Peabody Journal of Education*, *83*(2), 198–223.

Cronbach, L. J. & Snow, R. E. (1981). *Aptitudes and instructional methods: A handbook for research on interaction* (2nd ed.). New York, NY: Irvington.

Cuban, L. (2013). *Inside the black box of classroom practice: Change without reform in American education*. Cambridge, MA: Harvard University Press.

Culpepper, S.A. (2017). The prevalence and implications of slipping on low-stakes, large-scale assessment. *Journal of Educational and Behavioral Statistics*, *42*(6),706–725.

Cuypers, S. E. (2004). Critical thinking, autonomy and practical reason. *Journal of Philosophy of Education*, *36*(1), 75–90.

Darling-Hammond, L. (2010). *The flat world and education: How America's commitment to equity will determine our future*. New York, NY: Teachers College Press.

Darling-Hammond, L. (2013). *Getting teacher evaluation right: What really matters for effectiveness and improvement*. New York, NY: Teachers College Press.

Darling-Hammond, L., & McLaughlin, M. (1995). Policies that support professional development in an era of reform. *Phi Delta Kappan*, *92*(6), 81–92.

Davies, P. (2019). *The demon in the machine: How hidden webs of information are solving the mystery of life*. Chicago, IL: University of Chicago Press.

Dee, T. S., & Jacob, B. A. (2011) The impact of No Child Left Behind on student achievement. *Journal of Policy Analysis and Management*, *30*(3), 418–446.

Defeo, J. A. (2016). *Juran's quality handbook: The complete guide to performance excellence* (7th ed.). New York, NY: McGraw-Hill.

Dehaene, S. (2014). *Consciousness and the brain: Deciphering how the brain codes our thoughts*. New York, NY: Viking Penguin.

Deming, W. E. (2000). *Out of the crisis*. Cambridge, MA: MIT Press.

Deming, W. E. (2018). *The new economics for industry, government, education* (3rd ed.). Cambridge, MA: MIT Press.

DeRose, K. (2000). Ought we to follow our evidence? *Philosophy and Phenomenological Research*, *60*(3), 697–706.

Dewey, J. (1907). *The school and society*. Chicago, IL: University of Chicago Press.

Dewey, J. (1908). What pragmatism means by practical. *Journal of Philosophy, Psychology and Scientific Method*, *5*(4), 85–99.

Dewey, J. (1938). *Logic: The theory of inquiry.* New York, NY: Henry Holt.
Dewey, J. (1975). *Democracy and education: An introduction to the philosophy of education.* New York, NY: Free Press.
DeWolf, I., & Janssens, F. (2007). Effects and side effects of inspections and accountability in education: An overview of empirical studies. *Oxford Review of Education, 33*(3), 379–396.
Doll, R., & Hill, A. B. (1950). Smoking and carcinoma of the lung. *British Medical Journal, 2,* 739–748.
Duncan, A. (2010). Back to school: Enhancing U.S. education and competitiveness. *Foreign Affairs, 89*(6), 65–74.
Elgin, C. (2017). *True enough.* Cambridge, MA: MIT Press.
Engel, S., & Randall, K. (2009). How teachers respond to children's inquiries. *American Education Research Journal, 46*(1), 183–202.
Epstein, D. (2019). *Range: Why generalists triumph in a specialized world.* New York, NY: Riverhead Books.
Fantl, J., & McGrath, M. (2002). Evidence, pragmatics, and justification. *Philosophical Review, 111*(1), 67–94.
Fantl, J., & McGrath, M. (2009). *Knowledge in an uncertain world.* New York, NY: Oxford University Press.
Farley-Ripple, E., May, H., Karpyn, A., & Tilley, K. (2018). Rethinking connections between research and practice in education: A conceptual framework. *Educational Researcher, 47*(4), 235–245.
Feldman, R. (1988). Having evidence. In D. Austin (Ed.), *Philosophical Analysis* (pp. 83–104). Boston, MA: Kluwer Academic Pub.
Feldman, R. (2009). Evidentialism, higher-order evidence, and disagreement. *Episteme, 6*(3), 294–312.
Feldman, R., & Conee, E. (2005). Some virtues of evidentialism. *Veritas, 50*(4), 95–108.
Fernandez, M. (2012, October 13). El Paso schools confront scandal of students who "disappeared" at test time. *New York Times.* https://www.nytimes.com/2012/10/14/education/el-paso-rattled-by-scandal-of-disappeared-students.html
Ferreira, F., Baileyi, K., & Ferraro, V. (2002). Good-enough representations in language comprehension. *Current Directions in Psychological Science, 11*(1), 11–15.
Ferreira, F., Engelhardt, P., & Jones M. (2009). Good enough language processing: A satisficing approach. In N. Taatgen, H. Rijn, J. Nerbonne, & L. Schomaker (Eds.), *Proceedings of the 31st Annual Conference of the Cognitive Science Society* (pp. 413–418). Austin, TX: Cognitive Science Society.
Festinger, L. (1957). *A theory of cognitive dissonance.* Palo Alto, CA: Stanford University Press.
Festinger, L., & Carlsmith, J. (1959). Cognitive consequences of forced compliance. *Journal of Abnormal and Social Psychology, 58*(2), 203–210.
Finnigan, K., & Daly, A. (Eds.). (2014). *Using research evidence in education: From the schoolhouse door to Capitol Hill.* New York, NY: Springer.
Fisher, R. A. (1922a). On the mathematical foundations of theoretical statistics. *Philosophical Transactions of the Royal Society of London A, 222,* 309–368.
Fisher, R. A. (1922b). The goodness of fit of regression formulae, and the distribution of regression coefficients. *Journal of the Royal Statistical Society, 85*(4), 597–612.
Fisher, R. A. (1925). *Statistical methods for research workers.* Edinburgh, UK: Oliver and Boyd.
Fisher, R. A. (1935). *The design of experiments.* Edinburgh, UK: Oliver and Boyd.

Fisher, R. A. (1950). *Statistical methods for research workers* (11th ed.). Edinburgh, UK: Oliver and Boyd.
Freedman, D. (1987). As others see us: A case study in path analysis. *Journal of Educational Statistics, 12*(2), 101–128.
Freedman, D. (2009). *Statistical models and causal inference: A dialogue with the social sciences*. New York, NY: Cambridge University Press.
Friedman, O., & Turri, J. (2015). Is probabilistic evidence a source of knowledge? *Cognitive Science, 39*(5), 1062–1080.
Garrison, J., Podeschi, R., & Bredo, E. (Eds.). (2002). *William James and education*. New York, NY: Teachers College Press.
Gartner, L. (2012, July 23). Prince William teachers helped students on standardized tests. *Washington Examiner*.
Gerken, M. (2017). *On folk epistemology: How we think and talk about knowledge*. New York, NY: Oxford University Press.
Gigerenzer, G. (1989). *The empire of chance*. New York, NY: Cambridge University Press.
Gigerenzer, G. (2008). *Rationality for mortals: How people cope with uncertainty*. New York, NY: Oxford University Press.
Gillum, J., & Bello, M. (2011, March 27). When standardized test scores soared in D.C., were the gains real? *USA Today*.
Giroux, H. A. (2013). *America's education deficit and the war on youth: Reform beyond electoral politics*. New York, NY: Monthly Review Press.
Goodman, N. (1976). *Languages of Art*. Indianapolis, IN: Hackett.
Goodman, N. (1978). *Ways of worldmaking*. Indianapolis, IN: Hackett.
Goodman, N., & Elgin, C. (1988). *Reconceptions in philosophy and other arts and sciences*. Indianapolis, IN: Hackett.
Gopnik, A. (2009). *The philosophical baby: What children's minds tell us about truth, love and the meaning of life*. New York, NY: Farrar, Straus & Giroux.
Gopnik, A. (2016). *The gardener and the carpenter*. New York, NY: Farrar, Straus & Giroux.
Gopnik, A., Griffiths, T., & Lucas, C. (2015). When younger learners can be better (or at least more open-minded) than older ones. *Current Directions in Psychological Science, 24*(2), 87–92.
Gopnik, A., Meltzoff, A., & Kuhl, P. (1999). *The scientist in the crib: What early learning tells us about the mind*. New York, NY: William Morrow.
Gormley, W. T. (2017). *The critical advantage: Developing critical thinking skills in school*. Cambridge. MA: Harvard Education Press.
Grant, C. A. (2012). Cultivating flourishing lives: A robust social justice vision of education. *American Educational Research Journal, 49*(5), 910–934.
Hacking, I. (2006). *The emergence of probability*. New York, NY: Cambridge University Press.
Halpern, J. (2016). *Actual causality*. Cambridge, MA: MIT Press.
Hanson, N. (1958). *Patterns of discovery*. New York, NY: Cambridge University Press.
Hardin, G. (1968). The tragedy of the commons. *Science, 162*(3859), 1243–1248.
Hardwick, C., & Cook, J. (eds.) (1977). *Semiotic and signifies: The correspondence between Charles S. Peirce and Victoria Lady Welby*. Bloomington, IN: Indiana University Press.
Harris, D., & Herrington, C. (2006). Accountability, standards, and the growing achievement gap: Lessons from the past half-century. *American Journal of Education, 112*(2), 209–238.
Harris, P., Smith, B., & Harris, J. (2011). *The myths of standardized tests: Why they don't tell us what you think they do*. Lanham, MD: Rowman & Littlefield.
Hirst, P. (1975). *Knowledge and the curriculum*. New York, NY: Routledge.

Hoffman, J., Assaf, L. & Paris, S. (2001). High stakes testing in reading: Today in Texas, Tomorrow? *Reading Teacher, 54*(5), 482–492.

Holland, E. (2012, August 16). District finds widespread cheating at East St. Louis elementary school. *St. Louis Post-Dispatch*. https://www.stltoday.com/news/local/education/district-finds-widespread-cheating-at-east-st-louis-elementary-school/article_bad6a78e-e7d1-11e1-aa08-001a4bcf6878.html

Hume, D. (1993/1748). An *enquiry concerning human understanding* (2nd ed.). Edited, with an introduction by Eric Steinberg. Indianapolis, IN: Hackett.

Humphrey, G. (1924). The psychology of the gestalt. *Journal of Educational Psychology, 15*(7), 401–412.

Ijalba, E., Velasco, P., & Crowley, C. (Eds.). (2019). *Language, culture, and education: Challenges of diversity in the United States*. New York, NY: Cambridge University Press.

Inhelder, B., & Piaget, J. (1958). *The growth of logical thinking from childhood to adolescence*. New York, NY: Basic Books.

Jackson, C. (2018). What do test scores miss? The importance of teacher effects on non-test score outcomes. *Journal of Political Economy, 126*(5), 2072–2107.

Jackson, P. (2012). *What Is education?* Chicago, IL: University of Chicago Press.

Jacob, B. & Levitt, S. (2003). Rotten apples: An investigation of the prevalence and predictors of teacher cheating. *Quarterly Journal of Economics, 118*(3), 843–878.

James, T. (2019). *Elemental: How the periodic table can now explain (nearly) everything*. New York, NY: Abrams Press.

James, W. (1890). *Principles of psychology*. New York, NY: Dover.

James, W. (1975–1988). *The works of William James*. 20 Vols. (F. H. Burkhardt et al., Eds.). Cambridge, MA: Harvard University Press.

Janis, I. L., & King, B. T. (1954). The influence of role playing on opinion change. *Journal of Abnormal and Social Psychology, 49*(2), 211–218.

Jennings, J., & Rentner, D. (2006). Ten big effects of the No Child Left Behind Act on public schools. *Phi Delta Kappan, 88*(2), 110–113.

Jones, B. D. (2007). The unintended outcomes of high-stakes testing. *Journal of Applied School Psychology, 23*(2), 65–86.

Judd, A. (2012a, April 30). Cheating our children: Suspect scores put award's integrity in question. *Atlanta Journal-Constitution*. https://www.ajc.com/news/local/cheating-our-children-suspect-scores-put-award-integrity-question/tpmWyXz58D1Ai8wCamhqnJ/

Judd, A. (2012b, September 22). School test cheating thrives while investigations languish. *Atlanta Journal-Constitution*. https://www.ajc.com/news/education/school-test-cheating-thrives-while-investigations-languish/XAPhfpyjT6Zc0RCLOl9J4K/

Kahneman, D. (2011). *Thinking, fast and slow*. New York, NY: Farrar, Straus and Giroux.

Kane, T. & Staiger, D. (2002). The promise and pitfalls of using imprecise school accountability measures. *Journal of Economic Perspectives, 16*(4), 91–114.

Kelcey, B., Dong, N., Spybrook, J., & Cox, K. (2017). Statistical power for causally defined indirect effects in group-randomized trials with individual-level mediators. *Journal of Educational and Behavioral Statistics, 42*(5), 499–530.

Kelman, H. (1953). Attitudinal change as a function of response restriction. *Human Relations, 6*(3), 185–214.

King, J. E. (2017). 2015 AERA Presidential Address: Morally engaged research/ers dismantling epistemological nihilation in the age of impunity. *Educational Researcher, 46*(5), 211–222.

References

Kleinke, K. (2017). Multiple imputation under violated distributional assumptions: A systematic evaluation of the assumed robustness of predictive mean matching. *Journal of Educational and Behavioral Statistics, 42*(4), 371–404.

Kohn, A. (2015). *Schooling beyond measure and other unorthodox essays about education.* Portsmouth, NH: Heinemann.

Kohn, A. (2018). *Punished by rewards: The trouble with gold stars, incentive plans, A's, praise and other bribes* (25th anniversary edition). New York, NY: Houghton-Mifflin.

Koretz, D. (2005). Alignment, high stakes, and the inflation of test scores. *Yearbook of the National Society for the Study of Education, 104*(2), 99–118.

Koretz, D. (2008). *Measuring up: What educational testing really tells us.* Cambridge, MA: Harvard University Press.

Koretz, D. (2015). Adapting educational measurement to the demands of test-based accountability. *Measurement: Interdisciplinary Research & Perspectives, 13*(1), 1–25.

Koretz, D. (2017). *The testing charade: Pretending to make school better.* Chicago, IL: University of Chicago Press.

Kraft, M., & Gilmour, A. (2017) Revisiting the widget effect: Teacher evaluation reforms and the distribution of teacher effectiveness. *Educational Researcher, 46*(5), 234–249.

Kraut, R. (1990). Varieties of pragmatism. *Mind, 99*(394), 154–183.

Kuhn, T. (1970). *The structure of scientific revolutions* (2nd ed.). Chicago, IL: University of Chicago Press.

Kuhn, T. (1987). *Black-body theory and the quantum discontinuity 1894–1912* (a new edition of the 1978 book). Chicago, IL: University of Chicago Press.

Kvanvig, J. (2018). *Faith and humility.* New York, NY: Oxford University Press.

Labaree, D. (1997). Public goods, private goods: The American struggle over educational goals. *American Educational Research Journal, 34*(1), 39–81.

Ladd, H. (2017). No Child Left Behind: A deeply flawed federal policy. *Journal of Policy Analysis and Management, 36*(2), 461–469.

Ladson-Billings, G. (2006). From the achievement gap to the education debt: Understanding achievement in U.S. schools. *Educational Researcher, 35*(7), 3–12.

Ladson-Billings, G. (2016). And then there is this thing called the curriculum: Organization, imagination, and mind. *Educational Researcher, 45*(2), 100–104.

Lee, J., & Reeves, T. (2012). Revisiting the impact of NCLB high stakes school accountability, capacity, and resources: State NAEP 1990–2009 reading and math achievement gaps and trends. *Educational Evaluation and Policy Analysis, 34*(2), 209–231.

Levin, H. (2012). More than just test scores. *PROSPECTS: Quarterly Review of Comparative Education, 42*(3), 269–284.

Lindquist, E. F. (1951). Preliminary considerations in objective test construction. In E. F. Lindquist (Ed.), *Educational Measurement* (2nd ed., 119–158). Washington, DC: American Council on Education.

Linn, R., Baker, E., & Betebenner, D. (2002). Accountability systems: Implications of requirements of the No Child Left Behind Act of 2001. *Educational Researcher, 31*(6), 3–16.

Lipman, M. (2003). *Thinking in education* (2nd ed.). New York, NY: Cambridge University Press.

Littlejohn, C. (2012). *Justification and the truth-connection.* New York, NY: Cambridge University Press.

Magee, M. (2016, November 30). California's rising high school graduation rates subject of federal audit. *San Diego Union-Tribune.*

Manley, R., & Hawkins, R. (2010). *Designing school systems for all students: A toolbox to fix America's schools.* Lanham, MD: Rowman & Littlefield.

McDonnell, L., & Weatherford, M. (2016). Recognizing the political in implementation research. *Educational Researcher, 45*(4), 233–242.

McLean, J., & Ernest, J. (1998). The role of statistical significance testing in educational research. *Research in the Schools, 5*(2), 15–22.

Mendell, M. (1995). The problem of the origin of pragmatism. *History of Philosophy Quarterly, 12*(1), 111–131.

Menken, K. (2006). Teaching to the test: How No Child Left Behind impacts language policy, curriculum, and instruction for English language learners. *Bilingual Research Journal, 30*(2), 521–546.

Mercier, H., & Sperber, D. (2017). *The enigma of reason.* Cambridge, MA: Harvard University Press.

Merrow, J. (2017). *Addicted to reform: A 12-step problem to rescue public education.* New York, NY: The New Press.

Merton, R. (1973). *The sociology of science: Theoretical and empirical investigations.* Chicago, IL: University of Chicago Press.

Miller, G. (2003). The cognitive revolution: A historical perspective. *Trends in Cognitive Science, 7*(3), 141–144.

Misak, C. (2004). *Truth and the end of inquiry* (2nd ed.). New York, NY: Oxford University Press.

Misak, C. (2008). The reception of early American pragmatism. In C. Misak (Ed.), *The Oxford Handbook of American Philosophy* (pp. 197–223). New York, NY: Oxford University Press.

Misak, C. (2013). *The American pragmatists.* New York, NY: Oxford University Press.

Misak, C. (2016). *Cambridge pragmatism.* New York: NY: Oxford University Press.

Misak, C. (2018). Ramsey's 1929 pragmatism. In C. Misak & H. Price (Eds.), *The Practical Turn: Pragmatism in the British Long Twentieth Century* (pp. 66–84). New York, NY: Oxford University Press.

Mladenovic, B. (2017). *Kuhn's legacy: Epistemology, metaphilosophy, and pragmatism.* New York, NY: Columbia University Press.

Mlodinow, L. (2015). *The upright thinker: The human journey from living in trees to understanding the cosmos.* New York, NY: Pantheon.

Mlodinow, L. (2018). *Elastic: Unlocking your brain's ability to embrace change.* New York, NY: Pantheon.

Moore, G. E. (1959). A defence of common sense. In *Philosophical Papers,* pp. 32–59. London, UK: Allen & Unwin.

National Academy of Sciences. (2007). *Ending the tobacco problem: A blueprint for the nation.* (Richard J. Bonnie, Kathleen Stratton, & Robert B. Wallace, Eds.) Washington, DC: National Academies Press.

National Commission on Excellence in Education. (1983). *A Nation at Risk.* Washington, DC: U.S. Department of Education. https://www2.ed.gov/pubs/NatAtRisk/risk.html

Newell A., Shaw, J., & Simon, H. (1958). Elements of a theory of human problem solving. *Psychological Review, 65*(3), 151–166.

Nichols, S. C., & Sheffield, A. N. (2014). Is there an elephant in the room? Considerations that administrators tend to forget when facilitating inclusive practices among general and special education teachers. *National Forum of Applied Educational Research, 27*(1–2), 31–44.

No Child Left Behind Act. (2001). 20 USC 6311(b)(3)(C).

Noddings, N. (1994). *Educating for intelligent belief or unbelief.* New York, NY: Teachers College Press.

Norris, S. P. (1989). Can we test validly for critical thinking? *Educational Researcher, 18*(9), 21–26.

Norris, S. P. (1995). Format effects on critical thinking test performance. *Alberta Journal of Educational Research, 41*(4), 378–406.

Oakes, J. (2017). 2016 AERA presidential address: Public scholarship: Education research for a diverse democracy. *Educational Researcher, 47*(2), 91–104.

Osterlind, S. J. (2010). *Modern measurement: Theory, principles, and applications of mental appraisal* (2nd ed.). New York, NY: Pearson.

Osterlind, S. J. (2019). *The error of truth: How history and mathematics came together to form our character and shape of the world*. New York, NY: Oxford University Press.

Page, R. N. (2001). Reshaping graduate preparation in educational research methods: One school's experience. *Educational Researcher, 30*(5), 19–25.

Page, S. E. (2018). *The model thinker: What you need to know to make data work for you*. New York, NY: Basic Books.

Pasnau, R. (2017). *After certainty: A history of our epistemic ideals and illusions*. New York, NY: Oxford University Press

Pearl, J., & MacKenzie, D. (2018). *The book of why: The new science of cause and effect*. New York, NY: Basic Books

Pearson, K. (1900). *The grammar of science* (2nd ed.). London, UK: Adam and Charles Black.

Peirce, C. S. (1868). Some consequences of four incapacities. *Journal of Speculative Philosophy, 2*, 140–157.

Peirce, C. S. (1877). The fixation of belief. *Popular Science Monthly, 12*, 1–15.

Peirce, C. S. (1931–1935). *Collected Papers of Charles Sanders Peirce, Vols. 1–6* (C. Hartshorne & P. Weiss, Eds.); *Vols. 7–8* (A. W. Burks, Ed.). Cambridge, MA: Harvard University Press.

Pell, M. (2012). More cheating scandals inevitable, as states can't ensure test integrity. *Atlanta Journal-Constitution*, September 30.

Penrose, R. (2005). *The road to reality: A complete guide to the laws of the universe*. New York, NY: Knopf.

Peters, M., & Ghiraldelli, P. (Eds). (2001). *Richard Rorty: Education, philosophy and politics*. Towson, MD: Rowman & Littlefield.

Peters, R. S. (1966). *Ethics and education*. London, UK: Allen & Unwin.

Peterson, C., & Seligman, M. (2004). *Character strengths and virtues*. New York, NY: Oxford University Press.

Piaget, J. (1954). *The construction of reality in the child* (M. Cook, Trans.). New York. NY: Basic Books.

Plantinga, A. (1993). *Warrant and proper function*. New York, NY: Oxford University Press.

Plato. (2002). *Plato: Five dialogues: Euthyphro, Apology, Crito, Meno, Phaedo* (G. M. A. Grube, Trans.). Revised by John M. Cooper. Indianapolis, IN: Hackett.

Plato. (2004). *Republic* (C. D. C. Reeve, Trans.). Indianapolis, IN: Hackett.

Popham, W. J., & Ryan, J. M. (2012, April). Determining a high-stakes test's instructional sensitivity. Paper presented at the annual meeting of the National Council on Measurement in Education, Vancouver, BC.

Porter, T. (1986). *The rise of statistical thinking, 1820–1900*. Princeton, NJ: Princeton University Press.

Posner, B. Z. (1986). Individual's moral judgment and its impact on group processes. *International Journal of Management, 3*(2), 5–11.

Putnam, H. (1990). *Realism with a human face*. Cambridge, MA: Harvard University Press.

Putnam, H. (2002). Pragmatism and nonscientific knowledge. In James Conant and Urszula M. Zeglen (Eds.), *Hilary Putnam: Pragmatism and Realism* (pp. 14–24). New York, NY: Routledge.

Putnam, H. (2009). Dewey's central insight. In L. Hickman & G. Spadafora (Eds.), *John Dewey's educational philosophy in international perspective: A new democracy for the twenty-first century* (pp. 7–21). Carbondale, IL: Southern Illinois University Press.

Putnam, H. & Putnam, R. (1993). Education for democracy. *Educational Theory, 43*(4), 361–376.

Quine, W. (1953). *From a logical point of view*. Cambridge, MA: Harvard University Press.

Ravitch, D. (2010). *The death and life of the great American school system: How testing and choice are undermining education*. New York, NY: Basic Books.

Ravitch, D. (2020). *Slaying Goliath: The passionate resistance to privatization and the fight to save America's schools*. New York, NY: Knopf.

Reback, R., Rockoff, J., & Schwartz, H. (2011). Under pressure: Job security resource allocation, and productivity in schools under NCLB. NBER Working Paper No. 16745. Cambridge, MA: National Bureau of Economic Research.

Reeves, A. R. (2011). *Where great teaching begins: Planning for student thinking and learning*. Alexandria, VA: Association for Supervision and Curriculum Development.

Rolland, M. (2012, January 27). Cheating on Oklahoma exams leads to resignations, retesting. *The Oklahoman*, https://oklahoman.com/article/3643775/cheating-on-oklahoma-exams-leads-to-resignations-retesting

Rorty, R. (1982). *Consequences of pragmatism*. Minneapolis, MN: University of Minnesota Press.

Rorty, R. (1990). *Objectivity, relativism, and truth: Volume 1: Philosophical papers*. New York, NY: Cambridge University Press.

Rorty, R. (2015). Putnam, pragmatism, and Parmenides. In R. E. Auxier, D. R. Anderson, & L. E. Hahn (Eds.), *The philosophy of Hilary Putnam* (pp. 863–881). Chicago, IL: Open Court.

Rosenthal, R., & Jacobson, L. (1968). *Pygmalion in the classroom*. New York, NY: Holt, Rinehart & Winston.

Rosnow, R. L., & Rosenthal, R. (1989). Statistical procedures and the justification of knowledge in psychological science. *American Psychologist, 44*(10), 1276–1284.

Rothstein, R., Jacobsen, R., & Wilder, T. (2008). *Grading education: Getting accountability right*. New York, NY: Teachers College Press.

Rubin, D. B. (1974). Estimating causal effects of treatments in randomized and nonrandomized studies. *Journal of Educational Psychology, 66*(5), 681–701.

Rubin, D. B. (1976). Inference and missing data. *Biometrica, 63*(3), 581–592.

Rubin, D. B. (1981). The Bayesian bootstrap. *Annals of Statistics, 9*(1), 130–134.

Rubin, D. B. (2005). Causal inference using potential outcomes: Design, modeling decisions. *Journal of the American Statistical Association, 100*(469), 322–331.

Rutkowski, L., & Rutkowski, D. (2016). A call for a more measured approach to reporting and interpreting PISA results. *Educational Researcher, 45*(4), 252–257.

Ryan, A. (1995). *John Dewey and the high tide of American liberalism*. New York, NY: W. W. Norton.

Sapolsky, R. (2018). *Behave: The biology of humans at our best and worst*. New York, NY: Penguin.

Scheffler, I. (1973). *Reason and teaching*. New York, NY: Routledge.

Scheffler, I. (1974) *Four pragmatists: A critical introduction to Peirce, James, Mead, and Dewey*. New York, NY: Routledge.

Scheffler, I. (2009). *Worlds of truth: A philosophy of knowledge*. Hoboken, NJ: Wiley-Blackwell.

Schwartz, B. (1987). *The battle for human nature*. New York, NY: W. W. Norton.

Scriven, M. (1991). *Evaluation thesaurus* (4th ed.). Newbury Park, CA: Sage.

Siegel, H. (1998). Knowledge, truth, and education. In D. Carr (Ed.), *Knowledge, Truth and Education: Beyond the Postmodern Impasse*, (pp. 19–35). New York, NY: Routledge.
Siegel, H. (1999). What (good) are thinking dispositions? *Educational Theory 49*(2), 207–221.
Siegel, H. (2017). *Education's epistemology: Rationality, diversity and critical thinking.* New York, NY: Oxford University Press.
Sigmund, K. (2017). *Games of life: Explorations in ecology, evolution and behavior.* Mineola, NY: Dover.
Simon, H. (1954). Spurious correlation: A causal interpretation. *Journal of the American Statistical Association, 49*(267), 467–479.
Skinner, B. F. (1938). *The behavior of organisms.* New York, NY: Appleton-Century Crofts.
Slavin, E. (2002). Evidence-based education policies: Transforming educational practice and research. *Educational Researcher, 31*(7), 15–21.
Sokal, A., & Bricmont, J. (1999). *Fashionable nonsense: Post-modern intellectuals' abuse of science.* New York, NY: Picador.
Sosa, E. (2015). *Judgment and agency.* New York, NY: Oxford University Press.
Staffel, J. (2020*). Unsettled thoughts: A theory of degrees of rationality.* New York, NY: Oxford University Press.
Steup, M., and Neta, R. (2020, Spring). "Epistemology." *The Stanford Encyclopedia of Philosophy* (Edward N. Zalta, Ed.). https://plato.stanford.edu/archives/spr2020/entries/epistemology/
Stewart, A. (2014). How thalidomide works against cancer. *Science, 343*(6188), 256–257.
Stich, S. P., & Nisbett, R. E. (1980). Justification and the psychology of human reasoning. *Philosophy of Science, 47*(2), 188–202.
Stigler, S. M. (2016). *The seven pillars of statistical wisdom.* Cambridge, MA: Harvard University Press.
Stolley, P. (1991). When genius errs: R. A. Fisher and the lung cancer controversy. *American Journal of Epidemiology, 133*(5), 416–425.
Strauss, V. (2016). How can anyone take standardized test scores seriously when stuff like this happens? *Washington Post*, September 4, https://www.washingtonpost.com/news/answer-sheet/wp/2016/09/04/how-can-anyone-take-standardized-test-scores-seriously-when-stuff-like-this-happens/
Sturt, P., Sanford, A., Stewart, A., & Dawydiak, E. (2004). Linguistic focus and good-enough representations: An application of the change-detection paradigm. *Psychonomic Bulletin & Review, 11*(5), 882–888.
Sugai, G., & Tindal, G. (1993). *Effective school consultation: An interactive approach.* Belmont, CA: Wadsworth.
Suppes, P. (1970). *A probabilistic theory of causality.* Amsterdam, The Netherlands: North-Holland.
Takahashi, P. (2014, April 16). State investigation finds cheating at Las Vegas elementary school. *Las Vegas Sun*, https://lasvegassun.com/news/2014/apr/16/state-investigation-finds-cheating-las-vegas-eleme/
Taleb, N. (2007). *The black swan: The impact of the highly improbable.* New York: Random House.
Tarski, A. (1944). The semantic conception of truth: And the foundations of semantics. *Philosophy and Phenomenological Research 4*(3), 341–376.
Tattersall, I., & DeSalle, R. (2019). *The accidental homo sapiens: genetics, behavior, and free will.* New York, NY: Pegasus.
Thorndike, E. L. (1912). The measurement of educational products. *School Review, 20*(5), 289–299.

Thurston, D., McEachin, A., Penner, A., & Penner, E. (2015). Aiming high and falling short: California's eighth-grade algebra-for-all effort. *Education and Policy Analysis, 37*(3), 275–295.

Thurstone, L. L. (1925). A method of scaling psychological and educational tests. *Journal of Educational Psychology, 16*(7), 433–451.

Thurstone, L. L. (1934). The vectors of mind (Address of the president before the American Psychological Association, Chicago meeting, September, 1933). First published in *Psychological Review, 41*, 1–32.

Tienda, M. (2017). Thirteenth annual *Brown* lecture in educational research: Public education and the social contract: Restoring the promise in an age of diversity and division. *Educational Researcher, 46*(6), 271–283.

Tishman, S., Jay, E., & Perkins, D. (1993). Teaching thinking dispositions: From transmission to enculturation. *Theory into Practice, 32*(3), 147–153.

Tomasello, M. (2014). *A natural history of human thinking*. Cambridge, MA: Harvard University Press.

Tomasello, M. (2019). *Becoming human*. Cambridge, MA: Harvard University Press.

Toppo, G. (2013, April 11). Memo warns of rampant cheating in D.C. public schools. *USA Today*. https://www.usatoday.com/story/news/nation/2013/04/11/memo-washington-dc-schools-cheating/2074473/

Toppo, G., Amos, D., Gillum, J., & Upton, J. (2011, March 17). When test scores seem too good to believe. *USA Today*. https://usatoday30.usatoday.com/news/education/2011-03-06-school-testing_N.htm

Tversky, A., & Kahneman, D. (1981). The framing of decisions and the psychology of choice. *Science, 211*(4481), 453–458.

Tversky, B. (2019). *Mind in motion: How action shapes thought*. New York, NY: Basic Books.

Tyack, D., & Cuban, L. (1997). *Tinkering toward utopia: A century of public school reform* (rev. ed.). Cambridge, MA: Harvard University Press.

Unger, P. (2002). *Ignorance: A case for skepticism*. New York, NY: Oxford University Press.

Upton, J., Amos, D., & Ryman, A. (2011, March 10). For teachers, many ways and reasons to cheat on tests. *USA Today*. https://usatoday30.usatoday.com/news/education/2011-03-10-1Aschooltesting10_CV_N.htm

Vogell, H. (2011, June 6). Investigation into APS cheating finds unethical behavior across every level. *Atlanta Journal-Constitution*. https://www.ajc.com/news/local/investigation-into-aps-cheating-finds-unethical-behavior-across-every-level/bX4bEZDWbeOH33cDkod1FL/

Vygotsky, L. (1978). *Mind in society* (Vera John-Steiner, Ellen Souberman, and Michael Cole, Eds.). Cambridge, MA: Harvard University Press.

Wagner, P. A. (2009). Formalizing thinking for morally responsive administration. *Values and Ethics in Education*al *Administration, 8*(2), 1–8.

Wagner, P. A. (2018). Warranted indoctrination in science education. In Michael Matthews (Ed.), *History, Philosophy and Science Teaching: New Perspectives* (307–315). New York, NY: Springer.

Wagner, P. A., Johnson, D., Fair, F., & Fasko D. (2016). *Thinking beyond the test*. Lanham, MD: Rowman & Littlefield.

Wagner, P. A., Johnson, D., Fair, F., & Fasko D. (2017). *Focus on thinking*. Lanham, MD: Rowman & Littlefield.

Wagner, P. A., Johnson, D., Fair, F., & Fasko, D. (2018). *Thinking ahead*. Lanham, MD: Rowman & Littlefield.

Wagner, P. A., & Simpson, D. (2008). *Ethical decision making in school administration.* Thousand Oaks, CA: Sage.

Wagner, T. (2008). *The global achievement gap: Why even our best schools don't teach the new survival skills our children need—and what we can do about it.* New York, NY: Basic Books.

Wainer, H. (2009). *Picturing the uncertain world.* Princeton, NJ: Princeton University Press.

Weinrich, P. (2009). *Collective rationality.* New York, NY: Oxford University Press.

Wiley, R. H. (2015). *Noise matters: The evolution of communication.* Cambridge, MA: Harvard University Press.

Williamson, T. (2000). *Knowledge and its limits.* New York, NY: Oxford University Press.

Williamson, T. (2005). Contextualism, subject-sensitive invariantism and knowledge of knowledge. *Philosophical Quarterly, 55*(219), 213–235.

Williamson, T. (2018). *Doing philosophy: From common curiosity to logical reasoning.* New York, NY: Oxford University Press.

Winch, C. (2006). *Education, autonomy and critical thinking.* New York, NY: Routledge.

Wolgemuth, J., Hicks, T., & Agosto, V. (2017). Unpacking assumptions in research synthesis: A critical construct synthesis approach. *Educational Researcher, 46*(3), 131–139.

Wong, M., Cook, T. D., & Sterner, P. (2009). No child left behind: An interim evaluation of its effects on learning using two interrupted time series each with its own non-equivalent comparison series. Institute for Policy Research, Northwestern University, WP-09-11. http://www.ipr.northwesteni.edu/publications/papers/2009/ipr-wp-09-11.html

Woodall, M. (2015, July 25). Two more Philadelphia school officials finished by cheating scandal? *Philadelphia Inquirer,* https://www.inquirer.com/philly/education/20150724_Two_more_Philadel-phia_school_officials_finished_by_cheating_scandal.html

Woulfin, S. L., & Rigby, J. G. (2017). Coaching for coherence: How instructional coaches lead change in the evaluation era. *Educational Researcher, 46*(6), 323–328.

Wright, S. (1921). Correlation and causation. *Journal of Agricultural Research, 20*(7), 557–585.

Wright, S. (1983). Path analysis in genetic epidemiology: A critique. *American Journal of Human Genetics, 35,* 757–768.

Yeh, S. (2001). Tests worth teaching to: Constructing state-mandated tests that emphasize critical thinking. *Educational Researcher, 30*(9), 12–17.

Young, L. J. (2001). Border crossings and other journeys: Re-envisioning the doctoral preparation of education researchers. *Educational Researcher, 30*(5), 3–5.

Zhao, Y. (2018). *What works may hurt: Side effects in education.* New York, NY: Teachers College Press.

Index

abduction reasoning, 17–18, 36–37
absolute truth and evidence, 3–4. *See also* evidentialist approach to theory of knowledge; truth
accountability, 62–63, 115, 121–127
Achievement (Bradford), 7
Achinstein, Peter, 36, 47, 77
administrators. *See* pragmatic theory of knowledge; stakeholders at Level 2
alternative facts, x
Argyris, Chris, xvi
Aristotle, 41, 107, 109
artists' knowledge, 26
The Art of Logic in an Illogical World (Cheng), 71
assessment compared to evaluation, 87–88
assumptions, 20, 30–31, 36–37
Auerbach, David, 37, 79
authentic pragmatism, 60, 104
autonomy, 16

Baker, Lynne Ruder, 2
Bandura, Albert, 27
Bayesian strategies, 76, 77–78
Behave (Sapolsky), 89
behavioral approach to learning, 91–92
beliefs and truth, 1
Berliner, David, 56
best practices, 86
Beth, E. W., 15–16
biases, 123

Binet, Alfred, 107, 120
Bitwise (Auerbach), 37
bivariate distributions, 72
black-body radiation study, 5–6
Blackburn, Simon, xviii
black hole radiation example, 126
"black swans," 125–126
Bloom, Paul, 18, 90
Boltzmann, Ludwig, 72
Bradford, Gwen, 7, 23
Burge, Tyler, 7, 13, 17, 44
Burks, Barbara, 75–76, 77, 80, 89
Bush, George W., 53–54

Campbell, D. T., 48, 57, 65
carbon dating example, 113
Carlsmith, J., 93–94, 95
causation as not correlation, 73–77
cheating on standardized tests, 55–57, 65, 131–132
Cheng, Eugenia, 71
Chomsky, Noam, 92
cognitive dissonance, 93–94
cognitive entrenchment, xvi
collaboration, 118, 126–127
common ground, 115–116
Conee, E., 70–71
control groups, 73
correlation as not causation, 73–77
correlation coefficient, 72

correspondent theory, 6, 8, 34. *See also* realist theory of knowledge
counterfactual reflection/reasoning, 17–18, 80–81
Crick, Francis, xvi
culture, 17

Dane, Erik, xvi
Darling-Hammond, Linda, 56, 96
data interpretation, 108
deductive arguments, 36–37
Deming, W. Edwards, 54–55, 56, 65, 122, 133
Dewey, John, x, 36, 40–41, 47, 96
didactic instruction, 29
disagreements, 113–115
disciplines, varying skills for, 59
dogmatism in theory of knowledge, 44, 45
doubt, 10, 11, 19–20. *See also* skeptics and skepticism

Educating for Intelligent Belief or Unbelief (Noddings), 114
educational research. *See* evidentialist approach to theory of knowledge; stakeholders at Level 3
Educational Researcher, 88
efficiency, 88
egg packaging challenge, 63
Einstein, Albert, 72
Elgin, Catherine, 26, 36, 44, 47, 60
engineering school example, 63
epistemic demands of children, 18–19
epistemology: authentic pragmatism and, 34–35; caveats, 118; defined, ix, 10; difficulty of constructing, 6–7; disagreements about, 113–115; educational researchers and, 98–99; importance of, 60; learning instinct of humans, 20–21; needed for accountability, 14; need for excellence in approximating truth, 19–20; realism and, 16–19, 29; recommendations, 117–118; summary, 117; theory of truth compared to, 13–14; transducer caused disparity and, 38–39; as truth-seeking guide, 129–131; as unifying engine, 115–116. *See also* evidentialist approach to theory of knowledge; pragmatic theory of knowledge; realist theory of knowledge; truth
Epstein, David, xv–xvii
ESSA (Every Student Succeeds Act), 48, 53, 55, 57–59
evaluation: assessment compared to, 87–88; goal of plausible understanding, 98; knowledge theory and, 58–59; learning science *versus* program evaluation, 87–89; properly warrantable beliefs, 79, 81, 94–95, 96–97; testing concerns, 123–127; tools for, 18–19; value-laden nature of, 88–89. *See also* knowledge; stakeholders; standardized tests
Evaluation Thesaurus (Scriven), 87
Every Student Succeeds Act (ESSA), 48, 53, 55, 57–59
evidentialist approach to theory of knowledge: caveats, 82–83; correlation and causation, 73–77, 80; defined, 64, 76; evolution of, 120–121; getting things *rightly*, 69–71; inferencing and causation, 77–78; knowledge claims and, 91–94; as mirror image of pragmatism, 68; proper belief-basing, 70–74; radical skepticism criticism in, 70; recommendations, 82; smoking and lung cancer correlation, 74–76; summary, 81–82; truth and, 68–71, 81; warranting practices and, 79, 81. *See also* stakeholders at Level 3
existential angst, 103
experience, attention to, 41
Experience and Prediction (Reichenbach), 37

fast-thinking protocols, 60
Feldman, R., 70–71
Festinger, Leon, 93–94, 95
Fisher, Sir Ronald, 72–77, 80, 95
Flynn, James, xvii
Flynn effect, xvii
foundationalism, 8. *See also* realist theory of knowledge
future path forward: agreement among stakeholders to do no harm, 134–135; caveats, 138–139; recommendations, 137–138; stakeholders' common

concerns, 135–137; summary, 137

Galton, Francis, 72, 95, 107
Gaussian curve, 73
generalists, xv–xvi
geometry truths, 4
Gerken, Mikkel, 34–35
global achievement gap, 48
Goodman, Nelson, 26, 36, 42
Gopnik, Alison, 17, 18, 90
Great Conversations of Humankind: characteristics of, 25–26; collaboration and, 105; education and knowledge-seeking, 16; historical perspective, 101–102; learning sciences as foundation of, 90; preparing students for, xvi–xix; preserving meaningfulness of, 27–28; stakeholders agreeing to sustain, 135; students participating in, 117; teachers modeling, 27; tests and, 126–127; truth-seeking and, 24–25. *See also* Law of Figuring Things Out; truth

Hanson, Norwood, 121
Hegelian system-building, 40
Higgs boson, 38
"Horace Mann laws," 102
Houston Independent School District, 53–54, 55–56
"How do you know?" question, 1–2, 3, 9–10, 16–19, 68–71, 81
human learning instinct, 20–21
Hume, David, 69, 90

inauthentic pragmatists. *See* swaggerts
inductive arguments, 37
inferencing practices, 85
input subjectivity, 124
instrumentalism, 42
intellectual challenges, 50–52
internal realism, 8, 42. *See also* realist theory of knowledge
intersubjective agreement, 7–8

Jackson, Philip, 57
James, William, 34–36, 39–40, 41, 47, 68
justifications, standards of: stakeholders at Level 1 and, 108–109; stakeholders at Level 2 and, 110; stakeholders at Level 3 and, 110–113

Kahneman, Daniel, 104, 114
knowledge: as achievement, 7, 10; changes in, 94–95; evidence and claims of, 23–24, 91–94; evolving nature of, 47; importance of relationship with truth and reality, 15; as justified belief, 15–19; multiple-choice tests and, 14–15; realism and, 8; truth and, 70, 129–130. *See also* epistemology; truth
Knowledge and Its Limits (Williamson), 70
Kohn, Alfie, 93
Koretz, Daniel, 56, 57
Kuhn, Thomas, 5–6, 8, 44, 71, 91, 109

Law of Figuring Things Out: collaboration and, 117; intellectual tool for, 105–107; learning instinct of humans, 20–21; pragmatism embracing, 60–61; "slow thinking" and, 104; stakeholders' common concerns, 135–137; truth-seeking and, 22, 24, 104. *See also* Great Conversations of Humankind
learning, 20–21, 128–129, 132–133. *See also* evaluation; knowledge; truth
learning sciences, 89–90, 93, 95–97, 98
lies, 21–23
literature classes, 26
lucky guesses, 111–112
Luria, Alexander, xv

manifest error, 68
master truth-seekers, 27
memorization, xvi, 58, 59
Meno (Plato), 14
metacognition, 1
metaphysics, 34
methodology, 81, 82–83
Miller, George, 93
Mind in Motion (Tversky), 136
mineralogist example, 126
Mlodinow, Leonard, 90
Monopoly game example, 62–63
Moore, G. E., 69
moral and social challenges, 52
moral nihilism, 20
multiple-choice tests, 14–15, 31, 121, 123–125

A Nation at Risk report, 53
NCLB (No Child Left Behind), 48, 53–54, 54–57, 57–59
Necker, Louis, 107
Neta, Ram, 10
nihilism, 24, 45
No Child Left Behind (NCLB), 48, 53–54, 54–57, 57–59
Noddings, Nel, 96, 114
nongeneralists, xv–xvi
null hypothesis, 72

Oakeshott, Michael, 96
observation, 85, 93
Osterlind, Steven, 120–121

Page, Scott, 78
Paige, Rod, 53–54, 55–56
paradigm shift, 5–6
parents. *See* stakeholders at Level 1
Pareto frontier, 106
Pascal, Blaise, 72, 111, 118
path analysis, 75–76, 78, 80, 89
Pearl, Judea, 79–81. *See also* Bayesian strategies
Pearson, Karl, 72, 95
Peirce, Charles Sanders, 7, 35–40, 41, 47, 114
Peters, R. S., 96
Piaget, Jean, 15–16, 18
Plato, 2, 14, 41, 109
plausible claims, 34
pluralistic approach to justifying knowledge, x–xi
policy-makers. *See* pragmatic theory of knowledge; stakeholders at Level 3
pragmatic realism, 44
pragmatic theory of knowledge: authentic pragmatism, 34–35; breadth of, 50–52; caveats, 46; current focus, 42–43; evolution of, 119; founders of, 35–41; instrumentalism, 42; problem-solving compared to, 33; quest for accountability and, 122; radical skepticism criticism in, 70; recommendations, 45; "self-described," 47–48; shoot-from-the-hip problem solving compared to, 47–48; social constructionism, 43–44; stakeholders at Level 2 and, 49–53; summary, 45; truth and, 69; truth-seeking and, 131–132. *See also* Dewey, John; James, William; Law of Figuring Things Out; Peirce, Charles Sanders; stakeholders at Level 2; truth
prejudice, 123
principal at parochial school example, 50–52
probability, 38–39, 108
problem solving: defining challenges, 61–62; importance of understanding challenge, 60–61; rushing without understanding context, 58–59; shoot-from-the-hip answers compared to pragmatism, 47–48, 105–106; vanishing compared to being solved, 49–50, 51, 118. *See also* swaggerts
professional educational administrators. *See* pragmatic theory of knowledge; stakeholders at Level 2
Programme for International Student Assessment (PISA) tests, 56, 88
proper belief-basing, 70–74
properly based warrant, 79, 81, 94–95, 96–97. *See also* statistical strategies and results
prudent knowledge, 71
Putnam, Hilary, 2, 36, 42
Putnam, Ruth, 42

Quine, W. V. O., 36, 42

radical skepticism, 9–10, 11, 20, 21, 25, 45, 68
randomized controlled trial (RCT), 73–74, 75–76
Range (Epstein), xv–xvii
ratiocinate definition example, 111–112
rationality in search for truth, 44
Ravitch, Diane, 56, 96, 105
RCT (randomized controlled trial), 73–74, 75–76
realist theory of knowledge: epistemic demands of children, 18–19; goals of, 8–9; grounds for knowing, 7–9; internal realism, 42; knowledge and truth-seeking, 9–10, 15, 23, 29, 130; Kuhn and, 6; learners looking for, 13–14;

Plato and, 2; relativistic sharing and, 19–21; tools of, 16–19; world of senses and, 15–19. *See also* Great Conversations of Humankind; Law of Figuring Things Out; multiple-choice tests; stakeholders at Level 1
recipes, statistics as, 81, 97, 99, 134
recognition learning, 135. *See also* student building
reflective deliberation, 45
Reichenbach, Hans, 37
relativism, 6, 21, 28, 44
relativistic sharing, 19–21
religion and assertions, 47, 68
religious hypotheses about the universe, 39–40
representations, ordering of, 17–18
researchers in education field. *See* evidentialist approach to theory of knowledge; stakeholders at Level 3
Rhee, Michelle, 56, 59
Rorty, Richard, 36, 42, 43
Rubin, David, 80–81

Sapolsky, Robert, 89
saticficing approach of pragmatism, 34–35
Scheffler, Israel, 36
schooling responsibilities, evolution of, 102–105
Scriven, Michael, 87
senses as confirmation or disconfirmation, 15–19
Siegel, Harvey, 96
Simon, Herbert, 44
skeptics and skepticism: ancients and, 1–2; challenge of, 3–4; criticizing Level 1 stakeholders, 108; evidentialists and, 111–113; need for, 9–10, 28. *See also* doubt; radical skepticism
Skinner, B. F., 91–92, 95
"slow thinking" protocols, 60, 104
smoking and lung cancer debates, 74–76, 89
"snow is white" truth, x, 2, 109
social agreement, x
social constructionism, 4–6, 43, 45, 61, 94
social conventions, 97
social sciences, 120
social studies lessons, 27–28

sociopolitical contexts, 106
Socrates, 1–2, 14
Sokal, Alan, 5
"Some Virtues of Evidentialism" (Feldman and Conee), 70
specialization, xv
stakeholders: agreeing to do no harm, 134–135; disagreements among, 121–127; evolutionary sketch of, 119–121; importance of all levels of, 121. *See also* future path forward; stakeholders at Level 1; stakeholders at Level 2; stakeholders at Level 3
stakeholders at Level 1: caveats, 31; coaching students on tests, 56–57; Great Conversation of Humankind beginning with, 101; justifiable expectations, 108–109; recommendations, 30–31; researchers studying effectiveness of, 86–87; student building, xix, 127–129, 131–134; summary, 30. *See also* realist theory of knowledge
stakeholders at Level 2: as captains, 106; caveats, 65; as engineers, 107; historical perspective, 101; justifiable expectations, 110; needing competency and understanding, 60–61; recommendations, 65; responsibilities of, 106; subjective evaluations and, 121–124; summary, 64–65; swaggerts, 49–53, 61, 65. *See also* Every Student Succeeds Act (ESSA); No Child Left Behind (NCLB); pragmatic theory of knowledge
stakeholders at Level 3: about, xix, 64; approach to truth, 97–98; bifurcation, 86–87; caveats, 99–100; challenges, 103; evidence and knowledge claims, 91–94; evolution of, 102, 107–108; goals of, 85; justifiable expectations, 110–113; properly based warrant, 94–95, 96–97; recommendations, 99; similarities with other levels, 122; studying effectiveness of teachers, 86–87; summary, 98. *See also* evaluation; evidentialist approach to theory of knowledge; learning sciences

standardized tests: cheating on, 55–57, 65, 131–132; as mirage of objectivity, 29–30; multiple-choice tests, 14–15, 31, 121, 123–125; as nonpragmatic action, 48; teaching to, 62–63, 125. *See also* Every Student Succeeds Act (ESSA); No Child Left Behind (NCLB)

Stanford/Binet IQ test, 120

The Stanford Encyclopedia of Philosophy (Steup and Neta), 10

statistical strategies and results: as likely approximations of truth, 85; need for, 108, 111, 120–121; recipe comparison, 81, 97, 99, 134; truth and, 38–39. *See also* "How do you know?" question

statistics classes, 134

Steup, Mattias, 10

The Structure of Scientific Revolutions (Kuhn), 5–6

student building, xix, 127–129, 135

students, 63, 127–129. *See also* stakeholders at Level 1

subjective evaluations, 121–125

swaggerts, 49–53, 61, 65

sympathy, 90

Taleb, Nassim, 125

Tarski, Alfred, x, 2, 129

teachers. *See* stakeholders at Level 1

"teaching to the test," 62–63, 125

Terman, Lewis, 95

"test alignment," 62–63, 125

The Testing Charade (Koretz), 57

tests of significance, 72–73, 95

thalidomide, 103–104

theory of justification, ix–xi

theory of knowledge. *See* epistemology; evidentialist approach to theory of knowledge; future path forward; pragmatic theory of knowledge; realist theory of knowledge; truth

Thorndike, E. L., 95

Tomasello, Michael, 90, 119

Total Quality Management (TQM), 54, 65, 122, 133

transducer caused disparity, 38–39

triangulation, 78

True Enough (Elgin), 60

truth: caveats, 11; evidentialists as skeptical of, 102–113; focus on seeking, 117–118; as ideal, 1, 9–10, 21–23, 26, 108–110, 115–116; importance of relationship with knowledge and reality, 15; inferencing practices and, 85; knowledge and, 6–7, 70, 91, 129–130; master truth-seekers, 27; meaningfulness of, 23–25; pragmatists and, 47; rationality in search for, 44; realism and, 3–4; recommendations, 11, 30–31; as representation without error, 2–3; searching in antiquity for, 1–2; social constructionism and, 4–6, 43; summary, 10–11, 30; swaggerts and, 49. *See also* epistemology; Great Conversations of Humankind; knowledge; Law of Figuring Things Out; stakeholders

Tversky, Barbara, 136

uncertainty, 118

Unger, Peter, 10

unintended consequences, 46, 48, 118

validity, 36

Vygotsky, Lev, 29

Wagner, Nicole, 91–92

Wagner, Paul, 5–6, 8

Washington, D.C. schools, 56, 59

Watson, James, xvi

Williamson, Timothy, 16, 20, 69–70

Winner, Ellen, xvi

Wright, Sewall, 75–76, 77, 80, 89

Zagzebski, Linda, 96

zone of proximal development, 29

About the Authors

Paul A. Wagner is the senior ranking professor at the University of Houston–Clear Lake. He is chair of the Department of Leadership and Policy Analysis which includes all research methodologists, statisticians, and educational administrative faculty. He also holds a joint appointment in philosophy in the College of Human Sciences and Humanities. He has also taught management theory and organizational behavior for University of Houston–Victoria School of Business and consulted in evaluation and strategic planning in several major corporations and universities. He is a member of the American Philosophical Association, the American Psychological Association, and the American Educational Research Association. He has formerly served as executive secretary of the Philosophy of Education Society, and vice president of the Association of Philosophers in Education (a division of the American Philosophical Association). He has authored more than 100 publications including this one, his ninth book.

Frank K. Fair is a Distinguished Emeritus Professor in the Department of Psychology and Philosophy. He served for a number of years as coordinator of the philosophy program in the department, and he was managing editor of the journal *INQUIRY: Critical Thinking Across the Disciplines* from 2010 to 2017, when he retired from full-time teaching. His presentations and publications span a wide range of topics from issues in logic and philosophy of science, to survey research on the impact of post-tenure review policies in Texas and a consideration of affirmative action policies. He has written about Buddhism and Christianity in relation to modern science, and about to the need to listen to Plato in quality management. He is coauthor of a business fable about responding to change and leading innovation. But he especially values working with colleagues in education to replicate successfully the results of a Scottish experimental study in a Texas public school, showing that a Philosophy for Children program had a durable, positive impact on the cognitive abilities of a set of seventh graders that was still visible in the data when they were sophomores in high school.

www.ingramcontent.com/pod-product-compliance
Lightning Source LLC
Chambersburg PA
CBHW030139240426
43672CB00005B/185